M.A.P.S.
Parent's
Guide
to Teens

SHERYL MATNEY

MAPS: A Parent's Guide to Teens

First Edition

Published by 365 Press

www.lifemaps365.com

Cover & Interior Design : GKS Creative, www.gkscreative.com

Library of Congress Case Number: 1-7367186101

ISBN: 978-1-7338583-0-4 (paperback IS)
ISBN: 978-1-7338583-1-1 (paperback KDP)
ISBN: 978-1-7338583-2-8 (Mobi)
ISBN: 978-1-7338583-3-5 (EPub)

For media or booking inquiries, please contact:

STRATEGIES Public Relations
P.O.Box 178122
San Diego, CA 92177
jkuritz@strategiespr.com

Originally printed in the United State of America.

Dedication

To my parents,
for life.

To the counterpart,
Who made life with me.

To my kids,
Who bring life to me.

Table of Contents

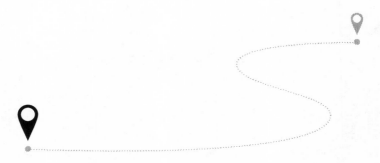

Introduction

I am an imperfect human being trying to do the best I can do in the present moment to bring purpose to my life. As an individual I am flawed, adaptable, serving, and loving. I embody various titles to many people as a mother, sister, daughter, niece, cousin, friend, co-worker, and confidant. I am most confident and proud in my role as a mother. From the very first premature day that my son Sam came into the world, the awareness of my responsibility and my role as a parent became a mission of critical importance to me. Not only did I realize that I had a lot of personal healing to acknowledge and conquer, but that everything about me would have some direct impact on him and ultimately all of my kids over a lifetime. That notion was a wake-up call that I continue to take seriously each day. In the early days after his birth, it was emotional, overwhelming, and traumatic. I matured immediately and began an evolution that formulated the basis for my concept of MAPS.

MAPS crystalized in my mind on a car ride home. I had just dropped my firstborn son, Sam, off at his first high school home-coming dance. Freshman through senior classmen swarmed the outside entrance as a line of cars, limos, and vans slowly circled through the drop-off area. It felt surreal to me. Leaving my son and his date in a sea of scantily clad, sexually charged, imbalanced maturity level, and varied street-savvy mass of high schoolers terrified me. How had I prepared him for such an experience? Would he be able to fit in and stand up for himself in such an environment? Unlike my homecoming dances, which were all held in the school gym, this current hotel venue felt way more like the real world. However, I did feel as though I landed in the middle of a teenage twilight zone. Both familiar and unfamiliar all at once. On my drive back home, a mental spin on what steps I had taken as a mother to help my son navigate life outside our home and town whirled as I drove. What steps do I follow to ensure that he will know which steps to take to find his own way? It was my own map of sorts, with ready access for every path in each new day. How will he know which way to go? He will know because I show, grow, flow, and go slow. I talk, confirm, connect, and repair. I am a map for him and I follow the way of model, adapt, participate, and slow down.

I am writing this book as a guide. It is filled with direct advice. It is full of stories and experiences. It is meant to be practical, supportive, entertaining, authentic, and enlightening. It is not a step-by-step how-to book. It can be picked up and read from beginning to end or referenced for specific suggestions within a particular topic. It can be introduced with success at any point in the relationship of parent to child. It can be applied in any demographic solely on the basis that the intention for good, healthy, open communication is the ultimate key. It does not assume that the information transcends the adequate means of a comfortable upbringing. It is merely my story and my way, which I believe is refreshing and helpful to those who seek it out. I wanted to write it because I think it is sound in practice. I have successful, fulfilling relationships with each of my three kids both collectively and independently. They are grounded, happy, motivated, loving people who strive to evolve. They teach me as much as I teach them, and they embody purpose, contribution, and care. They are the kind of people I want to seek out in the world.

The takeaway from this book is not the meaning of life, it is simply a way to live well. It promotes connection. It makes attempts at holism. It is a dream of mine. It is the culmination of fear, pride, work, insight, and desire. It is another baby of mine. It began in infancy. It will start with the teen years—a time of transformation, a bridge of sorts. It's my way through a twilight zone.

What is MAPS? MAPS is model, adapt, participate, and slow down. It's a method for life. MAPS is a guide and practice. MAPS is my mantra. MAPS is my acronym. MAPS is my philosophy. Not just MAPS for parenting but MAPS for life. Every day for 365 days a year, every year. It's a way to wake up each day and stay the course. I use MAPS to be the best version of me in each new day. Life MAPS365. Each new day to find the best way.

Model: this concept is key. It is the first practice of authentic living. What we say has no merit whatsoever if we do not model first and foremost. I can talk until I am blue in the face, but no words will ever say more than my actions. We are what we do, above whatever we say. We can proclaim that it is essential to "do as I say and not as I do." There is no merit in hearing a declaration and witnessing an opposing outcome. What is observed becomes just as viable of an option to what is heard. To achieve a level of success in raising teenagers, it is necessary to practice what you preach. This is a true statement with just about anything in life. Action manifests destiny. Model.

Adapt: the second concept. First, act well. Next, adapt right action to the appropriate environment. It is not purposeful to just model good behavior over and over and over with no awareness of how the good behavior meets the framework of environment. Some of the best actions will fall short if the circumstances don't lend well to the delivery. It would never make sense to give a fish a pair of shoes, even if they are brand new, designer label, awesome shoes.

It's great to be generous and giving but even more necessary to be altruistic. So, don't think that your teenager wants you to openly hug them and yell out, "I love you," in front of all their peers when you drop them off at school. The action and words are great ways to model to your teenager that you sincerely love them but are best adapted for delivery in genuine spaces and places. Let them openly know that you love them but let them guide the openness of the environment for exchange. Adapt.

Participate: this is the third concept and the pedal-to-the-metal key of MAPS. Without some level of participation, we will never truly connect with our teens. This means doing the work, not just declaring or spectating. Sit with them when they do homework, read a book to them out loud, watch a show that is a favorite of theirs, share personal stories, play a game, go to a performance of theirs, exercise together, run an errand for them, do whatever little thing that you can to show that you actively care. This concept lines up with modeling in that you have to do something and not just state it. It lines up with adapting in that it must be sincere in delivery, not just a rote practice of obligation. Participating implies engagement and engagement models a willingness to adapt. Get in on their level. It's not just about doing—it's how you deliver. Participate.

Slow down: the last and most simple concept. It is basic in its power and therefore simply overlooked. To connect with your teens well it is essential to not overbook. Do not overbook your life and do not overbook your teen's life. Fit in a time to slow down whenever possible. Make it a requirement. Just as we often impose an activity that our kids mumble and grumble about and then end up loving after they are required to take part, schedule downtime. I can't tell you how many times I received verbal push back when I would set a mandatory, Friday night game night with a home home-cooked meal and everyone home, at the table, and then playing games together or watching a movie together and it ended up being one of the best nights ever. Make memories, make laughter, be bored, take quiet time, teach family care and self-care. Slow down.

Who we are, as individuals—with our unique personalities, traits, behaviors, and habits— can often be misinterpreted by others. Even who we believe ourselves to be can become convoluted through interactions with others. We often subconsciously form our roles by bringing forth characteristics developed through our own families of origin. Such qualities are often defenses for our shortcomings and insecurities even if they feel positive and right. Since they can be so subconscious in nature, we may not realize that we are actually behaving in a manner inconsistent with our intentions. What we think is altruistic may actually be self-serving if we are not careful to consider or are not open to perspective. Often, as parents, we need to think on our feet just to survive a moment. Consideration and perspective are not naturally a part of action on the fly. This book is a clear, basic map of principles that act as landmarks for success for parents in action.

What follows first and foremost is a book of maps. Let MAPS become a set of principles rooted in form and function for every life situation on any path to discovery when raising teens. MAPS can be particularly helpful points for parents but can be used by all types of caregivers and mentors and will help to find some of the best ways through life in general. Success in parenting requires clarity, familiarity, and vision through a safe, efficient, tested route. The destination and journey may be personally unique, but the path is shared, tried and true. In any form of a roadblock, MAPS is a resource for consistent navigation. No location is unreachable with the right set of MAPS. The route doesn't have to always be smooth, it just has to be obtainable. MAPS will work. It is never too early to start defining a route with parenting practices. MAPS is also a guide for any stage and circumstance you wish. It can be used at any time in the parenting process. The idea is to follow MAPS to build a road with as little rerouting as possible. We are not looking for autopilot with the concepts but rather local back roads that you adopt because they are there for your best access. Be sure to add any pit stops and discoveries of your own. MAPS can be a wild ride. Enjoy the journey.

Realities of Parenthood

The role of parent manifests from the basic notion of starting a family. Most of the time the idea to become a parent is a conscious choice. Other times the role of parent is initially unexpected. You become a parent through the responsibility of rearing a child. So, it follows that being a parent means to responsibly raise a child or children. Unfortunately, this is not always the case due to the fact that many of us who are now parents were raised in dysfunctional families. Dysfunction is easily passed along through generations if we choose not to acknowledge the habits and effects we grew up with and instead follow the same patterns. We can be the most responsible, focused, and loving parent and inadvertently create major dysfunction by placing our personal shortcomings, expectations, erroneous beliefs, and ineffective cycles on our kids. We may look in the mirror but we only see what we want to see.

Perhaps a clear approach to parenting well involves a look at our kids instead of a look in the mirror. When we look at our kids we remove our own egos. When we look in a mirror we are either hypercritical of the image or fooled by the fleeting reflection. Our kids are generally a more accurate and consistent reflection for us.

Blocking our own ego is not always easy. A good parent will strive in the highest manner possible to have the best intentions of the child in mind. Such a goal requires a lot of personal introspection, healing, and evolution especially if we carry dysfunction from our own families of origin. For me the mirror came the second my first son was delivered into the world. I have not stopped looking inside myself for ways to grow as a whole person to be the best parent possible for my kids.

When my son Sam was born, he came into the world six weeks early. I thought I had more time to get ready for him, but I did not. My water broke in the middle of the night and I was taken to the hospital where everything was set up to give him the best fighting start into the world. Once he was delivered, I was only allowed to touch his hand. He was whisked away from me and put into an incubator for eleven days. I was not allowed to hold him until three days after he was born. All of my great plans for nursing were relegated to pumping milk for bottles, every three hours like clockwork. Ironically, those first eleven days of his life were the start to many conversations with him about everything and anything. The hours that I sat with him I would verbally and melodically explain that I was his mother, that he was so very loved, that he came early, was in the hospital, and was being well taken care of by everyone around him. I would talk about how God loved him, how his parents loved him, how his grandparents loved him, and then verbally list all the details of the day and moments that were taking place around him and for him. I would sing to him "You Are My Sunshine" to break up the conversations, just so he could hear the sound my voice and know that I was near. When it finally came time to bring him home I continued the practice of talking and singing. I believe the conversations set boundaries for success with both of us. From those early narratives there was a clear message about what was going on in his life and mine, and it created a secure foundation. I think that open, honest, sincere communication is the best approach to parenting, hands down. My number one job as a parent, outside of meeting their most basic needs, is to talk with my kids about everything.

I was hit with severe postpartum depression after Sam was born. I did not know what it was initially, I just knew that it took every ounce of will to get me out of bed to take care of him properly. I didn't know a lot in those first few months. I was overwhelmed, battling my brain, sleep deprived, and traumatized. Having a newborn was none of the bliss that I imagined at first. It was super hard work! I called all of those closest to me with infants and cursed them for not warning me about the realities. I tell all new parents-to-be that the greatest blessings of a child are mixed with the makings of a personal world turned upside down. Know this going into it and be ready. Navigate. My best advice is to begin by laying a path filled with communication, rhythm, and care. Talk with your kids about everything. Meet their most basic needs. Add fun. Be present.

It's a challenge to parent well in today's world. I say it is important to be present, yet we have nothing but distractions and devices competing with our time. Cell phones and computers, though they seem to connect us relationally, are actually very isolating. The use of cell phones inhibits verbal interaction and communication. The use of social media fabricates authentic perspective on life and relationships. We have access to so much more in the sense of opportunity, discovery, tangibility, and convenience but we also compromise physical connection, integrity, and personal development by stifling how, where, and to whom we show up. We allow devices to make us lazy without realizing the detrimental effect it can have on relationship in our lives. We live in a big, wide world, but our habits can make it small and stunted. In addition to devices and social media access, there is a whole new set of issues we face today as parents, with legal and illegal substances. The dangers of drugs are much greater today than they ever have been before. We need to be aware of how easy it is for our kids to be exposed to and gain access to marijuana, opioids, and everything in between. It has become so socially acceptable to use drugs in all kinds of new and different ways. We cannot be complacent about any of the issues surrounding raising teens in this current day and age.

How will you know if you are on the right path in raising your children? It should start with following practices that are proven to work successfully. It goes without saying that each person is unique—both parent and child. So, if every person is an individual then we need a set of guidelines that will get us to common ground no matter what each person brings to the table. If we want to arrive at a desired end point, but each person needs a different means for finding the way, how do we parent the differences? This is where the concept of MAPS works so well. We can use MAPS to obtain a desired outcome when the route may be slightly different for each child. If we are modeling desired behaviors as parents, actively listening to the needs of each child, participating in the lives of our child, and slowing down with and for our child then it doesn't matter if we have a power child, type B child, or anything in between, the concept applies, just the personality differs.

So, the key to great parenting becomes a melding of responsibility, altruism, and guiding principles. With MAPS you can navigate all of it well. The end point is yours to establish and the journey there is one where everyone involved will want to take part. Figuring out the destinations and finding the way will be all the fun if each member stays engaged through the ride. It's like defensive driving . . . go with the flow, but be aware of your part, too. One of the greatest compliments I once received was from a therapist who knows much about my story, my goals, and my core being through past sessions. Because I apply and manifest the process of MAPS as a parent, with raising and interacting with my kids, I found function. He told me that my family—my three kids and I—are a functional family who make mistakes. If we intend to raise healthy, successful children, we must be healthy and successful adults. We may believe we are healthy and successful, but we should strive in the highest manner possible to block our own egos when we look in the mirror or our kids reflect a mirror for us. It goes back to determining if there is dysfunction or function with mistakes. Nobody is perfect, but if our guiding principles are grounded, conscious, and rooted in integrity then we can have faith that even through our own mistakes and shortcomings we can achieve positive success in parenting.

ROAD MAPS

Break the cycle of dysfunction through modeling behavior and healthy, open communication.

Do the personal work necessary to model behavior you desire to pass on to your kids.

Be clear and present when you engage with your kids.

Provide structure in the best way possible by creating a rhythm for living that works for your family, fostering personal growth, and creating safe boundaries for care.

Make personal relationships core. Don't rely on fun and technology, or take present moments for granted.

Become educated on and be aware of the myriad issues facing teens in the current day and age by maintaining an open exchange of information, asking questions, and encouraging ongoing dialogues.

Honor individuality by adapting to and adopting multiple ways to achieve various paths to the same or similar end.

Be positive, even when you don't always feel like it on the inside.

Puberty

If you are ever caught off guard by the unfamiliar with your kids, it is a safe bet to blame it on some aspect of puberty. The only certainty in puberty is that each of our children will experience the changes puberty initiates. The challenge is that no one child will go through the experience in the same way. As a parent, this can make puberty one of the most difficult aspects of raising teens to navigate. The good news is that there is a framework of characteristics, ages, and stages for puberty that help parents recognize and adapt to the onset and progression of hormonal changes in our teens. There are multiple keys to success in this topic area but the critical piece is in creating safe space during the entire experience.

To begin, openly communicate about puberty prior to or at onset and help the child drive the dialogue. A great way to initially broach the subject is at the same time that puberty is discussed in schools. Most public and private elementary schools discuss the topic of puberty through health education in or around the fifth grade. Some type of communication goes home to families announcing the subject, outlining the school's approach, and disclosing the date the subject will be presented. Parents usually have to give permission by signing a form and can generally request access to the curriculum. This is a great way to bring up the topic with your kids without making them feel singled out. Discuss the communication that comes directly from the school. Let your child know that you know what is being discussed and when. Additionally, let them know that you will follow up with them after the lesson is presented for their own benefit. Then, ask them if they have specific thoughts, concerns, or questions as they approach the lesson. Keep everything lighthearted and straightforward. Let them know and help them feel that you are coming from a place of understanding because puberty is something we all go through. It is important, as a parent, to recognize symptoms, stereotypic and otherwise, and to not take things personally as our children change through the process. Keeping a sense of humor, letting go of our "babies," not taking things personally, and openly discussing sensitive, uncomfortable topics are all keys for success.

In most cases, when kids start to go through puberty they have absolutely no idea what it is and what is going on within themselves. I remember several conversations with my crying daughter where she would be talking and then through sobbing tears she would announce in stutters, "I don't even know why I am crying!" Then she would continue with a floodgate of emotion and cry and cry. I would simply state that it was okay for her to cry and not know why she was crying. I think it is so necessary to validate the feelings, even if they can't be defined, because just as the kids don't know what is going on inside them, we may not recognize what is happening at first either. It is important to just accept the emotion for what it is in and of itself. A lot of times we define so much through childrearing as our kids go through the toddler and preteen years, because we are essentially aiding in teaching and cognitive development. Steps, method, and explanation in those early years are key for understanding. Puberty is often not that clear. It is as much emotional as it is physiological. Oftentimes our children will seek meaning by definition from us, but what will truly serve is support and understanding in presence alone. Proximity, support, and connection without cause/effect explanation may be a better anecdote. Our children will subconsciously search for comfort without specifically knowing why. They may even revert in behavior that doesn't seem age appropriate. They will feel weird, act weird, and be weird in a manner that may not feel comfortable to anyone in the family at first. They will need us to pause, proceed with caution, and be present. Puberty is a roller coaster of change and everyone will need to ride it out.

I remember clearly the day my oldest, Sam, went to his fifth grade health education talk on puberty. We did just as I suggested above as parents and discussed the communication that came home, outlining the program. We sent him off to school that day reminding him of the event, letting him know we would be thinking about him, asking him to keep in mind any questions he may have that didn't get answered, and to be ready to discuss the subject after school. His dad and I sat down with him together later that afternoon and we talked with him about the presentation. We asked him to share what he thought about the discussion, how other classmates acted, what questions were asked, and how the delivery went in general. He gave us a clear picture and nothing stood out as unexpected or inappropriate. We asked him if he had questions of us on anything specific that was confusing or unclear. He told us that everything seemed pretty clear with the exception of one question. He mentioned that they talked a lot about body changes, and anatomical parts and explained the fertilization process of an egg from a female and sperm from a male to make a baby. What he didn't get, and what was not explained to the class, was how the egg and sperm come together so fertilization can take place. So, I took the lead and let him know about male and female body parts fitting together so, the man is joined with the woman during an act of lovemaking to produce a child, and that is how the sperm and the egg connect. When I was done explaining things as clearly and directly as possible, he paused for a minute, looked right at me, and announced, "Huh, I never would have guessed that!" It is one of those precious "kid" moments that will stay in my mind forever. I tell the story to this day, for a good laugh, whenever the occasion merits.

When my younger son, Shaun, went through the same health discussion four years later, we had a similar before and after conversation with a bit of a been-there-done-that stance. As a result, I did not wait for his dad to return home when going through the question and answer, I just started talking in the car on the way home. Sometimes with Shaun you have to seize the moment to get a full and open response. He gave similar feedback as his older brother regarding the questions, behavior of other classmates, and content of material. I told him that Sam had one question after his presentation and it was related to how the sperm and egg came together. I asked Shaun if he was unclear as well. I let him know that it is important to be able to come to us, for any reason, to ask questions. It doesn't ever matter if it is me or his dad who respond to the questions. I let him know as parents, we would always keep each other in the loop and follow up individually if necessary. I then explained the scenario, as I did for Sam, on how men and women come together to make babies. He was much less expressive than Sam, but had a similar curiosity and surprise about the explanation of the physical act. Overall, it was another successful conversation. His dad did follow up with him later that day, after I filled him in on my part, and we closed the loop.

My daughter, Sarah, is the middle child, and was given the same talk with very similar results. In addition to the standard delivery, we talked about periods, bras, and emotions. For better or for worse, she actually had several experiences with coming-of-age incidents that I would never choose to take on at the age she was exposed, but that we conquered head on as they came our way. The first few were mild, and mostly related to girls in school and the different rates in which breasts develop. She had a couple stories about bras being hung from the lockers of girls who had large chests early on. There were stories of girls who were not wearing bras, when perhaps it may have been prudent to cover smaller breasts sooner rather than later. The discussions mostly centered around modesty, curiosity, and the effects of bullying on girls who are not having open discussion with their families and are left to their own devices. We always asked Sarah to be open with sharing her knowledge and perspective when appropriate and to support her friends and herself in the best way possible.

We let her know, too, that girls are much more susceptible to advances from boys and men early in the development process because of hormones, desires, the media, and access to pornography in the current day and age. We had a mini scare with her when she woke us up in the middle of the night, dreaming and talking in her sleep, around the age of eleven. She was thrashing around, crying and calling out, "Don't touch me, don't touch me!" in her sleep. She woke me quickly and I was at her bedside listening to her calling out as my heart sank and I was sick inside. I woke her from the dream and sat with her to calm her. I tried to uncover the dream with her and draw out a bit from what she had said. She was pretty out of it and felt vulnerable and scared. I didn't push too much, but as a parent I had feelers up and began racking my memory of times when she had sleepovers, playdates, classes, activities, and the like where unknown happenings were always possible.

The next morning her dad and I spoke with her about any situations away from home where she may have felt exposed or uncomfortable with anything unusual regarding her body, safety, and appropriate touch. She was a little overwhelmed and unsure of what we were getting at and neither of us felt right as parents just leaving it alone. It was such a specific and unexpected exclamation that spoke out in her dream. I scheduled a doctor appointment for her with our female pediatrician. When we went in together, I explained the situation and the result was a pap smear for my eleven-year-old daughter. The outcome was that everything was intact and fine, with no signs of any trauma. I share this story because as parents we must be on guard in every way. It is always right to take action for your child in situations that are extreme, because you don't really know what they are being exposed to when they are out of your care. Even when they are in your care, a lot can happen that may be surprising and/or wrong. Always advocate for your child to the best of your ability.

Another premature happening with our daughter came at a birthday party a couple of years later. She was at a friend's house for a thirteenth birthday party. It was a sleepover at their home with a pool, Jacuzzi, and huge backyard. Her friend had an older brother and family friends who were invited as well. The next day, after my daughter arrived home, my girlfriend who hosted the party called to let me know that she had something unsettling to share. My girlfriend said that when she walked by the Jacuzzi, where my daughter was with a bunch of other girls, her age and older, she heard my daughter say, "Oral sex." When she stopped and asked my daughter, "What did you say?" Sarah responded in embarrassment by saying, "Oh, nothing," at which everyone started laughing. I was stunned by the call and told my friend I would talk with my daughter and get back to her.

I sat down with Sarah to discuss the phone call, and asked her if anything unusual happened in the Jacuzzi at the birthday party. I let her know that I was told something that concerned me and asked if she had any idea what it might be about. Sarah let me know that the girls were talking in the pool with a couple of girls who were two years older than the birthday group. The girls in the birthday group were middle schoolers (seventh and eighth grade), and the older girls were high schoolers (tenth grade). One of the older girls was a sibling of a girl in Sarah's grade, and she and her friend were trying to share how much they knew about what all of the boys and girls in high school were doing with each other. They mentioned a boy, who was friends with Sarah's older brother, and a girl who together were having oral sex. When Sarah listened to the story, she recognized the boy's name and she asked the girl, probably somewhat loudly since they were all in the Jacuzzi, "What is oral sex?" It just so happened that the question was asked when my friend was walking past the girls. Therefore, Sarah was blamed for an innocent action that seemed to be much worse than it was on her part.

The older girl was gossiping to act cool, and my daughter was trying to piece together a story to share with her brother, but she had no idea what it was that was being declared. So, I had to take on the task of explaining to my thirteen-year-old daughter the definition of oral sex. I approached it matter-of-factly, as information that would arm her with knowledge when other kids start to talk about it and act on it inappropriately. I let her know that it is first and foremost and intimate act that should be shared only by committed, loving, monogamous couples, as in marriage, per our family belief system. I explained that it can sound gross, is taken way too lightly as an act not always categorized as sex, can be demeaning and degrading if done under the wrong circumstances, and should never be forced on anyone. I told her she would understand it better in the future at more age appropriate times. I asked her if she had any questions. She didn't at the time because I honestly think a lot of it went way over her head. Later in her high school years, I brought up the story when she was talking with me about her concern for some girls in her grade who were performing oral sex in the backyards of friend's parties—ironically, one of the brothers of the girl who originally told the story in the Jacuzzi was the person involved in the act with my daughter's friend. When I recalled the prior conversation to draw a parallel, my daughter had no recollection. Again, all of this to share that it is always appropriate to arm your children with specific knowledge due to circumstances. They will take in just what they need at the time and leave the rest behind. The brain will process only what it can, in the best way needed for each situation.

The stories above highlight the winding ways of puberty. As I mentioned in the beginning, no two kids go through puberty in the same way. Puberty is somewhat of a journey— both for the person going through the process, those around them, and the family. For this reason, it is important to participate as the best strategy from MAPS. Puberty is an active process that can involve many twists and turns to a destination that leaves behind a familiar place. Once you travel through puberty, you never return to the point of entry. This means that active participation is critical in order to not lose the way with your kids. Step in with personal stories; understanding; presence; clarification; and open, lighthearted conversations. Talk with boys about issues that girls may go through and girls about issues that boys may go through. We had talks with our boys about bras, periods, and emotions so they would have some knowledge of subjects that will affect them indirectly in the long run. Participate by engaging and supporting rather than ostracizing.

Both of my sons began to spend a lot of time in the bathroom "taking a dump" more than once a day. Reach out first by asking if they are feeling okay. If you are sensing a pattern, acknowledge awareness by pointing out that it is normal for bodies to get the best of us with different feelings and changes. This means they know you have insight, can relate on a certain level, care to pay attention, and are open to support—not chastise. All of that sets a baseline for discussion and connection. Seek the advice of other parents if need be. We raised our kids in the Catholic faith and knew an amazing family in our church with great parents and awesome kids who were a few years older than our own. We talked with the father of the family and asked advice on how he broached the subject of masturbation with his boys. Knowledge can be power. Participation can make all the difference surrounding puberty. Don't be afraid to tackle the concept of masturbation with girls as well. A conversation on this topic came a little later for us with my daughter, but it is important to address nonetheless. In all cases I suggest open dialogue . . . not necessarily graphic explanations of individual, physically charged matters. Address openly the awareness and physiological realities, but include prudent ways to understand and navigate.

I ended up calling back my girlfriend and explaining the outcome of my discussion with my daughter regarding the birthday party happening. It actually helped my friend bring up the subject with her own daughter. Everything went well and a pattern for openness with uncomfortable topics was set among my friends in general from that point. I share stories all the time with my friends so they know that transparency most often equals success. If you participate then your kids will seek you out as an ally. Nothing is better than aligning yourself with people you love.

ROAD MAPS

One of the most important points to emphasize with puberty is to pay attention. Although every child takes a different path, there are parameters in age to help parents gauge unfamiliar behavior and habits. What seems out of the blue and uncharacteristic can certainly be frustrating and unexpected but if it catches you as such then evaluate the situation. In doing so, place emphasis on timing, circumstance, and support rather than labeling or a need to understand the occurrence. Participate first by presence. If overreaction on either side presses to the surface take some time to deduce. Sometimes a focus on the reaction from our perspective can help shed light on the catalyst for behavior from our kids. Our reactions may stem from the fact that we feel as though we are losing control when in fact that may be exactly the issue coming from our teen.

Paying attention to the situation as a whole automatically removes any egocentricity that may prevent participation. Participation may simply mean that you choose not to act out and just offer to be available. I remember several conversations with my daughter where she would simply state that she didn't need my opinion—she just wanted me to listen. Listening is participation. One-on-one time is participation. Sitting next to someone when they cry is participation. Communicating awareness and acceptance without calling someone out is participation. It may be a little draining at times, but it doesn't have to be complicated. Remember and relate. Puberty is the defining component of the teen years—we have no other choice than to participate.

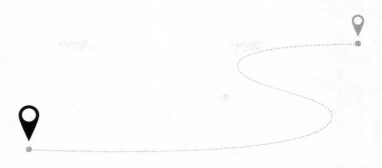

Dating

Dating is a hot topic between parents and kids and it seems to me that perspective plays the biggest role in whether or not a child should have a boyfriend or girlfriend. Most kids want to start dating as soon as possible. Most often, crushes begin in primary grades when children are in a school environment, away from home, with mixed genders and new faces. As children grow up they subconsciously strive for autonomy from their family of origin and gravitate to a range of personalities that offer comfort, rebellion, confidence, adventure, and ultimately personal connection. They are able to do this, relatively unsupervised, and it can be a very healthy way to develop and mature into individual young adults.

Parents bring their own set of experiences to the table, and usually have very specific views on restrictions to dating and relationships for their kids. I have found that a set age to begin dating can both entice the child to do otherwise and restrict foundations to form healthy, balanced relationships. I feel I am well versed to speak on the subject of dating because I have both male and female children. I have experiences as a single, dating adult; a married person;

and a divorced person, newly back in the dating world, post kids. My own first kiss took place in a Jacuzzi, at age fifteen, in a forced situation during a cheerleading initiation with a seventeen-year-old football player. My first real kiss and boyfriend followed in the fall of my junior year at a very shy age sixteen. It happened much more the way that I wanted it to the second time I had a first kiss, but I was navigating all unfamiliar territory. I had two more boyfriends before graduating high school and left for college insecure and unprepared to take on new, young adult relationships, let alone a huge new world outside the confines of my hometown. My own parents did not have specific parameters for my dating, nor did they ever talk about relationships other than their own. They grew up in the same neighborhood, were high school sweethearts, married just before my dad graduated college, and started a family within months of getting married. It was a fairytale story to me and I was the good first child, so I tried desperately to forge a similar path when it came to my own dating relationships. It seemed innocent enough when I was at home, but once away at college I did not have the knowledge or confidence to carry out a relationship in the way I would want my own kids to be able to today.

As a result, my take on dating may appear to be progressive on the surface. I believe it is sensible, conservative, and grounded. The basis for my dating rules is rooted in age appropriateness and definition. The term boyfriend/girlfriend is extremely broad based. As a label, it can take on a specific weight in the sense of relationship, but it doesn't have to be that way. I have learned that it is just as appropriate for my kids to have a boyfriend/girlfriend in seventh grade as it is for them to have one in tenth grade—what differs is the definition of the label and what they can do in relationship in seventh grade versus tenth and beyond. With each relationship my kids wanted to explore we opened conversations, educated about parameters, became familiar with all parties involved (parents and the mate), and set boundaries. It's like calling body parts by their defined names; at first, to a younger child, it may seem embarrassing but the more often you do it, the less uncomfortable it becomes. Over time there is no sensitivity because you are informed, knowledgeable, and it shapes as a straightforward, practical fact that doesn't carry any stigma, second-guessing, or figuring out. The same is true of relationships. When each stage builds appropriately over time what develops is an intrinsic sense of respect, awareness, feelings, and confidence that can all be a healthy, straightforward process. I do not have personal family experience in anything other than heterosexual relationships but I believe these guidelines are the same across the board. The concept of MAPS supports my premise no matter the coupling.

From a child's perspective, relationships carry all kinds of meaning and feeling. From a first crush to an exclusive, long-term commitment and everything in between, there are a whole host of influences that initiate couples. Kids start to learn what attracts them to another, both internally and externally. They may gravitate to an opposite attraction to fulfill areas they may lack in their own personalities. Or, they could be motivated by the attention of peers when they make choices about who they find attractive. They can secretly pine away over someone for years without ever acting on it and later realize the person continues to meet their secret desires. Conversely what seemed wonderful in someone at the time may later be nothing like what they want. They may also simply just have feelings, desires, and attractions for another because of proximity, family ties, chance circumstances, and mutual admiration. Whatever the case may be, it's likely that they will have experiences with others in relationship that match multiple versions of such definitions. It is all a healthy process of development in growing into themselves.

In the early years they are seeking affirmation and over time a curiosity of hormones and feelings mix in to create desires that are worth honing. It is a huge area of explorations that can often take over rational thinking. Their bodies can often trump their minds and in the moment with a person they are attracted to what may seem right is later realized not to be true. The other danger in this for kids is the exposure to alcohol and drugs that could inhibit clarity and conscience in various situations with persons they are attracted to or find themselves with by circumstance. It is a vast world of choice with many moving parts that don't always work together well. Again, kids can often think they know much more about relationships than they really do. It can also be that they want to appear to know more than they do for their peers. Since many children develop at different rates it can also be challenging to know when they are supposed to be keeping up with their peers and when it is okay for them to stand on their own timing with their own attractions. It can be over-whelming in so many different ways. Ultimately I think they want to be able to safely explore different avenues, with different mates of their choosing, to feel like they are getting what they desire. The heart rules, but it is the head that needs to be kept in line to understand appropriate experimentation. Our kids need to know that they are making right choices about desires for another and they need to be taught discipline and control as well.

As parents this is an arduous task in the sense of balance, safety, and values. It requires a lot of energy to stay on top of the feelings and desires of our kids. We have to teach them how to recognize feelings and how to behave appropriately at the same time. What we want is control over their relationships, and we should have it on the highest level, but we also have to teach them how to choose to behave wisely so that they can learn self-control internally. Often-times as parents we want to set specific designations for what we think is best for our children. We want restrictions on age for having a boyfriend/girlfriend because we assume they are just always going to be in over their heads if they start too young. We take our own experiences and we want our kids to do the same as us or something quite different. Relationships are so very individual so, as parents, maybe we are called to guide and monitor, but not define. It's a fine line. As parents we need to keep our kids safe. We don't want them to get in over their heads with a mate and have it end up altering a great life path filled with opportunities that may not otherwise happen if they mess things up by not thinking or by being hasty and unlucky. It's a great responsibility to have as a parent and one that is not to be taken lightly. So, what are we to do? If we pry we may generate secretiveness. If we allow too much freedom there can be grave consequences. I think education is the best answer. Education, conversation, participation, and adaptation are necessary by both the parent and the child with adaptation being the main focus in the concept of MAPS.

Sam met a girl during his eighth grade year of middle school. They sparked an interest with one another riding up and down the elevator together. She had injured her leg playing soccer and was on crutches. As a result she had access to an elevator key and needed help carrying her books. It was cool to be able to ride the elevator with someone who had access, so Sam acted as the gentleman by carrying the backpacks and they struck a connection through the repeated rides from the first to second floors. It was a cute and innocent beginning of a friendship. I started hearing through the grapevine that Sam had a girlfriend, and I honestly don't remember which one of us broached the subject first. I remember him telling me he wanted her to be his girlfriend and what followed were a handful of conversations discussing and defining the meaning of "girlfriend" to a thirteen-year-old. The definition at that age consisted of hanging out together in mostly supervised environments—either at her house or at ours. They were not allowed to be in their bedrooms alone together and since neither could drive, all the time they spent together outside of school was coordinated with parents. They were allowed to kiss, hold hands, and sit close together, snuggle up while watching TV, and the like. We had these conversations repeatedly, as check-ins, between mother and son and among my other kids as well. It was dinner conversation material—the best forum for open discussions—on the parameters of such a relationship so all involved would have a clear idea of boundaries as they grew and took interest in potential suitors as well. The definition of girlfriend was mostly a label at that age but it meant a lot for Sam to have a defined girlfriend nonetheless.

The relationship between Sam and the girl lasted for over a year in this capacity. When they first began dating, the girl was a local resident, but she lived on a nearby military base. This was nice because access to her home was not automatic; it had to be coordinated by parents for him to get on the property. My home was generally supervised because I was usually always around during lunches and after school hours. Later on in the course of their courting, her father retired from the military and they bought a house in a different suburb, which helped keep time spent together very balanced and coordinated among all the other activities and friends in an eighth grade world. We were very lucky as a family to have a dating standard set up in such a way that it evolved into a healthy example of dos and don'ts under practical conditions.

In addition to discussing the parameters of ages and stages of relationships we were able to talk as a family about cell phone use, texting, and proper use of all online technology surrounding teenagers this day and age. We had dinner table talks about the appropriate use of texting, which was not granted to my son when he first started dating the girl, but happened the summer prior to his freshman year of high school when they were still together. We talked extensively about how if you would not say something to someone's face then it should never land in a text message. I would make my son call voice to voice to coordinate plans with the girl and her parents so I could be involved in some of the details and to get him comfortable with communication skills in general. We discussed appropriate use of photos and how he was never allowed to take a picture or receive a picture without clothing in any way or something he would not want his parents or grandparents to see as a measure. Young, innocent relationships are a great way to open so many lines of communication with your kids. Plus it honors their feelings, builds bonds of trust, openness, honesty, and teaches choices, actions, and consequences. Almost every teen situation can be modified as a teaching point for a range of ages—as I mentioned, my younger kids were reaping the benefits of all the talks and parameters for their own evolution.

Sam ended up taking his girlfriend to his first high school formal—which was actually the catalyst for my book. I shared the story of feeling like I was in the twilight zone when I dropped them at the homecoming dance and the concept of MAPS was born on my ride home. With the rubric of MAPS active in our home, when it came time for my son to act on his decision to break off and end the relationship with the girl, he knew that it was something that he was going to have to do face-to-face. Since the girl lived in a different city from ours, I drove him to her house. We planned together that I would stay in the car near the girl's home so that when he finished talking to her he could leave the house and know that he was free to go. Such an endeavor is never an easy process, no matter the side you are on. It was a big lesson for him and one that we all grew through together. It was not an easy or a straightforward process because of the various emotions and feelings of each party involved. Again, we talked about all of it as a family—great life lessons to share and experience.

It was almost two years before he took interest in another girl as a girlfriend. It never really transpired into a relationship but he did end up taking her to a formal dance. In January of his senior year of high school he took interest in a girl whose family had been connected to ours through other siblings and friendship for years. They began dating prior to a spring formal that year and are together to this day, even though they have had to weather long distances. As far as I perceive from my conversations with my son and my exposure to them as a couple, it is a healthy relationship. It is one that I believe my son has a level of confidence and trust that he can appropriately navigate with his girlfriend because he has been able to adapt and build through his other experiences with girls where MAPS lay the foundation.

My daughter, Sarah, began a great relationship with a local boy whose family we have known for years. His older brother is Sam's age and they were in kindergarten together. The family lived behind us, their house facing one street and ours another. I never knew the boy who Sarah was dating except that he was a member of the family; I knew the dad, mom, and older son as more than acquaintances but not as friends we would socialize with regularly. Sarah had several classes over the years with the boy and began to date him the summer before her senior year of high school. They dated through the rest of high school and into most of the first year of college (in separate states), in what I feel was a healthy, grounded relationship.

Sarah, as I may have mentioned before, is an extremely mature child, who is rooted in her belief system and stands for strong morals and values. She can really hold a line, better than any teenager I know, and as a result has had a lot of hardships test her at an early age because she tends to be a mirror to her peers that they often don't want to look into or know how to face. She is sensitive, compassionate, rigid, strong, caring, hardworking, and open about who she is, what she believes, and who she wants to be as she evolves into an independent, young adult. She, like me, for better or worse, believes in fairytales, is a hopeless romantic, and wears her heart on her sleeve. It is because of all of these traits that I have the utmost of confidence in her in every way. I have seen her consistently display such unwavering character and it makes me so proud because I know she has already far surpassed where I was developmentally at her age.

This is mostly a good thing, but in one occurrence within her relationship with her boyfriend I took note of the fact that I am her parent, and despite her maturity level at eighteen, she is also young and vulnerable with all the other teenage attributes mixed in. Since she often displays such consistency and rarely, if ever, gives me something to worry about, I was careless in how much I put on her shoulders. As parents we are called to be smart and aware for our kids so they can learn to be smart and aware for themselves. Adaptation from MAPS is the mantra here, but participation with all of its facets is also key. There are many ways to participate with our kids in the general sense of activities, homework, outings, one-on-one time, etc., yet participation is also taking a proactive role in staying in the heart of what our children are doing from an adult, life-experience perspective.

On New Year's Eve, my daughter, being the romantic at heart, wanted to do something special with her boyfriend—they both wanted to. Since my daughter does not drink, or like to go to high school "parties" per se, they made plans for themselves only. The idea was to go to the baseball clubhouse, play board games, eat yummy snacks, and drink Martinelli's apple cider to ring in the new year. It sounded like a fun, easy, innocent time to me—one that I wanted to live vicariously through them because I happened to be alone for New Year's Eve that year. They came by my house to grab all of the goods. Her boyfriend had access to the clubhouse because he was on the varsity baseball team. The baseball field was next to an elementary school, on the outskirts of town in a neighborhood. I think it was the idea of being in their own little world that was exciting. A unique little venue of which no one else would be a part.

Again, I let them go without hesitation—not concerning myself with the expectation of a holiday "adventure" or the fact that it was just the two of them and that the location was slightly remote.

Quite honestly all of those factors should've been in the forefront of my mind. I am the parent, called to be vigilant for my kids when they are not thinking of big-picture scenarios. The night went well enough. Their curfew was 1:00 a.m. for the special circumstances, yet in retrospect even that was a risk because legal curfew in our town is 11:00 p.m. if under the age of eighteen, and both my daughter and her boyfriend were seventeen at the time. I go to sleep in my bedroom when I am tired, close the door, and keep my cell phone by me. I never sleep on the couch to wait up for my kids. My house is so small, less than one thousand square feet, and I am a light sleeper, so I usually hear when they arrive home. If I don't, I generally wake up in the middle of the night to use the restroom and I check in to see they are safe. If something ever happened, I have my phone next to my bed, so I would wake to a call as a last resort, if they needed me.

She arrived home by curfew that night and I woke to her coming home, got up to acknowledge her, hugged her, and went back to sleep. We talked the next day about the night—she shared details and it sounded fun. Looking back I could tell she was a little quieter than normal, but I knew too that she was tired from staying up. A day or two later we were in the car, headed somewhere together as we often do as mother/daughter, and it came out that she had been uncomfortable with the seclusion of her New Year's Eve plans. Nothing bad had happened, but minor lines were crossed intimately that she did not feel comfortable with under the circumstances. Two grounded, connected, healthy, happy people do not always equal success at the age of seventeen. Boys stereotypically have a lot of external peer pressure to "perform" with girls and on top of that there are raging hormones promoting such desire for actions as well. On top of that, being in an exclusive relationship with someone to whom you are attracted to, as a teenager, spurs desire, feelings, and curiosities that may feel natural yet can quickly spiral out of control.

Oftentimes, teenagers are ruled by their hormones and hearts and not their heads. As a parent we need to account for and counsel on such a fact. I had dropped the ball and mistakenly put too much credit on my daughter's black-and-white part of her personality. Her boyfriend was caught in the moment, the pressure of a holiday and his physical feelings. My daughter was under extra pressure to maintain her lines while in a "remote" place, caught up in the moment and her own curious desires. She drew her boundaries, definite for sure, but not exactly comfortable. She was disappointed by the ease of potential progression and down on herself when she should have been chastising my support of the event. I recognized quickly that it is my role to be more sensible and less romantic for her and to play the "bad cop." I needed to admit that I dropped the ball. I can have the utmost confidence in my girl, but mix the situation with her boyfriend, who I really only know through her, put the two of them together alone, and I am called to mitigate.

We ended up having a great conversation about the whole scenario. A lot of good came from the different subjects we were able to broach. She needs to learn that there is a whole world of influences that do not make her a bad person because she doesn't always meet them in certain confines. She realized that she can ask to lean on me, and that just because she is consistently strong doesn't mean that I am not going to say "no" when I feel a situation may be inappropriate. It was a great lesson for her boyfriend because she shared the details of our conversation and was able to let him know I was going to be monitoring the environment more closely and revealed the importance of respect despite inquisitiveness and peer pressures. Nothing bad or major happened, just subtle lines were blurred, but the realization to all parties involved, including me, was that it could've been a perfect scenario for much risk and regret. I am thankful for these lessons. They are challenging because they shine a light on human nature and vulnerability. When we face such lessons with an open spirit and mind, we evolve in health, connection, and insight that serves us well. It creates a continued environment of trust, support, and adaptation that keeps us actively moving forward.

My final message is that adaptation isn't just simply accepting an activity in your child's life. It doesn't just mean orchestrating either. There are areas in our kids' lives where we need to knowingly insert ourselves whether they want us to or not. Adaptation is always going to be a two-way street, not just accepting as I first imagined. My awareness on this component of MAPS extended as a lesson from my daughter that I have to adapt for her and participate with her as a parent simply because I know better. It's a version of "because I told you so" but it is not condescending. It is tried and true life experience that is imposed on one level, yet acknowledged as alignment.

ROAD MAPS

Don't get caught up in making set rules for dating. The message with dating and teens is to adapt by setting appropriate boundaries. Both of my boys had a girlfriend in their preteen years but that only meant that they had a friend that they liked exclusively who happened to be a girl. It didn't mean anything more than a simple attraction for one girl in particular. Both of my boys had girlfriends as seniors in high school, in which case the label was a very different set of boundaries. Work with your kids. Adapt through conversation, respect, enforcement, education, consequences, and relationship with all parties involved. Learn from mistakes. Advocate for your kids. Support by being aware. Get to know all the people involved in relationships with your kids. Communicate with boyfriends and girlfriends just like you would your own kids so that everyone is on the same page.

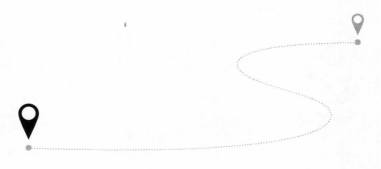

Driving

We get through the challenges of teaching our kids how to sleep through the night. We get through the challenges of helping our kids learn how to eat. We get through the challenges of guiding our children through learning to walk, potty training, tying shoes, dressing themselves, etc. We begin to think in many respects that we have the whole parent-as-teacher thing down, and then we have to help teach our kids how to drive. All of the latter tasks require patience, consistency, discipline, modeling, and practice but they generally take place within a controlled environment. Welcome to the open road! Not only do we need to offer support, but when teaching our kids to drive we literally put our lives in their hands. It is humbling to teach your child how to drive and when approached successfully we should be empathetic and rise above, not seek to control or condescend. Learning how to drive is not an easy task for anyone. If as a parent you feel you are not ready to take it on, there are plenty of options to have an instructor do the work for you. I recommend making such a choice if your personality is not up to the task of staying calm. There is no harm in recognizing when it makes more sense to use a trained professional. It is also important to note our own driving habits and make sure that we don't pass on bad habits that come from years of not thinking much about driving skills at all. The best advice from the perspective of MAPS is to adapt as parents when teaching kids how to drive.

The milestone of reaching the age to get a driver's license is an exciting time in the life of a teen. It is often marked by counting down the exact days to the age of fifteen and a half so a driver's license can be obtained on or super close to the date of the sixteenth birthday. Most teenagers are determined to start driving as close to the age of sixteen as possible. Others are not as motivated for various reasons and that is fine, too. There does not have to be a set expectation for when a driver's license is obtained unless there is a necessity where driving independently requires the motivation to act as soon as legally possible. If that is not the case, then act when the timing is most comfortable for your teen.

There are online options for the permit exam, which both of my sons used to study, log required hours, and ultimately print the certification necessary to go to the DMV and take the test. My daughter chose to sign up for an all-inclusive program that walked her through the process each step of the way. Her course definitely provided a more detailed experience when it came to truly learning the rules of the road. She also passed all of her tests on the first attempts, which I would attribute partially to her choice in program. I would say the unique choice to make in getting a permit and license is in deciding when the timing is right. No one person has the same time frame as another unless it's to map out the days to the exact birthday. Learning how to drive is a process and takes patience and confidence. To be in control of deciding when to start is a great way to own the responsibility and take initiative. If the financial aspect of driving instruction and the like comes from the parent then it may make sense to let all the other decisions, outside of when to start, form as mutually agreed upon. Anyone who has gone through the steps already will have beneficial input too—so ask around.

One of the main challenges of teaching kids how to drive is the scare factor. It is scary to not be in control of a car as the passenger of a new driver, and it is scary to send your kids off in a car alone, as a new driver, once a license is successfully obtained. Just because a driver's license is issued, doesn't equate to success with driving, it equates with success of passing the driving test. I liken it to standardized testing in the sense that a score mostly reveals how well you took the test, not necessarily a direct measure of intelligence or overall knowledge. What really makes the difference in level of knowledge is exposure to subjects, ideas, facts, and repeated input and development. The same is true with driving. In order to be a good driver, you need to repeatedly drive under various conditions, circumstances, and environments. You have to practice how to be aware, defensive, patient, and decisive at the same time that repetition with driving forms muscle memory and a level of comfort that becomes learned over time. In order for this to happen parents have to let kids drive.

There were so many times when it would have been much quicker, less stressful, and super straightforward for me to drive somewhere instead of letting my new drivers drive. Bite your tongue, trust the process, and let your kids drive. Learn to do this initially during the training phase. Take your kids to a wide-open space when they first get behind the wheel of a car. Give a concise overview of the basics, put them behind the wheel, give them a chance to drive around where there is no risk of accident and bite your tongue. I am going to say it again (and again)—bite your tongue. No one learns how to drive well if a parent is yelling, criticizing, forcefully directing, or repeating statements over and over about what to do. Use a calm voice and slight guiding hand movements and nothing more. I don't care if you're exploding inside, keep it under control. Learning how to drive is intimidating at first; no one needs to be dealing with an intimidating parent on top of it all.

I know it is easier said than done because I have taught three kids how to drive, so I also know that it can be done despite the fear and submission going on inside of me. I survived every situation that felt like was going to instantly result in an accident or side swipe or crash—it's all about perception without control, and as parents, that is what we are called to conquer through the experience. It's the instinctual lack of ability to control when someone else is in the driver's seat and the lack of control fuels the perspective that really is not as bad as it seems. The child will self-correct before it's too late if we give them the surrender they deserve. This is true, like I mentioned above, of post-driver's license driving as well. Sam had been driving for several months with his own license. I realized quickly that having an extra driver in the house was a huge benefit in many ways. He would love to run to the grocery store for me in a pinch, or pick up his brother from friend's houses or his sister from soccer practice. A lot of my busywork time was freed up due to his willingness to drive just about anywhere in those early days. Mostly all of the errands he would run for me were relatively straightforward routes either in town or with short freeway rides on familiar roads.

One day he came to me and asked if he could drive himself to a retreat center for the weekend where he was to be volunteering as a group leader. My initial reaction was to blurt out a "no" because it was not a straightforward route and there were options to carpool. After talking about the request together he let me know that he wanted the flexibility of his own car and I had no strong reason for not wanting him to drive other than my own peace of mind from worry. We discussed the route, the spotty cell phone coverage in places, the remote location, and some of the tricky turns and roads. I realized through our conversation that it was a good opportunity for him to familiarize himself with a different driving experience with controlled risk. He was headed to a group of people who were anticipating his arrival. It was not a super far drive at seventy-five minutes yet it was longer than a standard trip around town. It was close enough that if anything happened we could get to him without complication. It was a great chance for both of us to grow from our parent/child relationship. He would be taking on more independence and I would be trusting him as a young adult. The trip was a success all around and it led to other opportunities with future trips for him. He is currently on a road trip across the country, as a twenty-year-old as I write these words. He and his girlfriend are trekking her car from San Diego to Clemson University where she will be attending college in the fall. They are having the time of their lives as they explore different cities and travel America's highways. I am not worried about his driving. He checks in by phone a couple times a day and I am happy for the adventure he is creating along the way. He never would've gotten to this comfort zone with his driving if we both did not trust each other along the way and adapt within our fears, worries, desires, and expectations.

My daughter, Sarah, had a similar experience as a new driver. I am not going to lie when I say I was more worried about her venturing out on a mini road trip alone than I was about her brother. It's not that I don't have confidence in her ability. I believe I had more trust at the time in her driving skills than I did of her brother's. It's just the risks of a female being stuck somewhere alone are greater than those of a male being stuck. I think it is important to recognize such a fact but not to set up limits purely on the fact of female risks. I want to model for and teach my daughter to be empowered and aware. It is important to me that she feel and believe in the fact that she can do the same things that her brothers can do but that she may just need to be more aware of specific details for safety. In the case of driving it seems to me that a female is more vulnerable to potential attack if stranded on the side of the road, so paying attention to how to mitigate circumstances may be slightly more important for her. The idea of planning a route, having access to safety and protection devices, cell phone coverage, and roadside car assistance are all necessary components to consider and especially so for females.

We were planning a trip from San Diego to Palm Desert, where one of my best friends from high school has a second home we all love to visit together. We often meet on the weekends for a quick, fun, mini vacation. One weekend we planned a trip but my boys had activities that were limiting our time together a bit and my daughter did not have the same restrictions. She wanted to leave early and stay longer than my two boys. We were going to end up taking two cars so we could accommodate everyone's schedules yet it still turned out that my daughter had the most time of all of us. She requested to make the trip with the first car on her own and have us join her the next day. I was initially leery as the drive winds through some remote back hills, roads, and turns, some of which have broken cell phone coverage and no place to access immediate help if the car breaks down. My friend was already at the desert home on the day my daughter wanted to travel so someone would be waiting for her arrival, and she was proposing to travel during midday with plenty of daylight and active cars on the road. She wanted the time to herself to think, listen to music, and gain confidence in mastering a road trip of her own.

She also wanted the one-on-one time with my friend as they have a close relationship, much like she is his adopted daughter. All of my kids feel a very strong bond to my friend Stephen and do feel like he is a surrogate parent—someone they enjoy time with, can count on, ask advice of, and spend quality, fun, meaningful time with whenever possible. We all look forward to our trips together. Sarah wanted this to be extra special time for the two of them and she and Stephen were planning to go dress shopping for her upcoming prom. She made the trip alone, went shopping for a prom dress, and enjoyed a great night on her own with Stephen. The whole adventure gave her confidence and formed a special memory as well.

I always worry as a parent until I know a safe arrival takes place, and the whole experience reminds me how important it is to encourage development for and with my kids and not to restrict them because I feel fearful of them venturing out on a trek that I don't have control over. It's a tough pill to swallow initially, letting them go off outside my parental comfort zone. Yet it's my job to help form them into confident adults and that requires faith in letting go of my own fears about general life risks out in the big wide world. The only way they can become healthy, grounded, contributing, compassionate, well-rounded adults is if I let them grow into their fullest potential by fostering and supporting their appropriate hopes, dreams, and desires. Part of that process means supporting independence.

Driving becomes a piece of the independence puzzle through adaptation. Incrementally we send our kids out into the world in a very structured, controlled manner. We take them to activities, lessons, classes, and well-monitored environments. Eventually they participate in getting themselves from point A to point B by walking, biking, carpooling, busing, and the like. Then they eventually reach driving age and we as parents lose a great deal of control. Not just through the process of helping them learn to drive, but in letting them take the car on their own, drive around other family members and friends, and ultimately go off in a car a farther than typical distance without us. It is through adaptation within MAPS that we teach our kids to "fly." It requires a great deal of letting go on the part of the parent and it is crucial that we quite literally put our kids in the driver's seat.

As my third child is currently going through the process of driving with his newly acquired permit he is very aware of how the adults around him are treating the experience of driving with him. Even when comments are not verbally resounded he still picks up on the tension of how passengers hold themselves when he is on the road. It is for this very reason that we are called to adapt in every way outside our comfort zone to foster confidence in our new drivers. It speaks to trust and even a little to humility. It plants seeds of capability in our teens as we hand over the reins. It is one of the most clearly demonstrated tasks of handing over power to our kids, of genuinely placing ourselves in their hands. As our children become successful drivers our level of adaptation will benefit us by allowing our kids to shoulder more of the responsibilities in everyday life with us.

My mantra for parents teaching teenagers to drive is "Bite your tongue!" On top of that I say, "Breathe!" It is a proven fact that breathing—a big breath in the nose and out the mouth—will actually lower levels of stress. It helps us pause. Being quiet and breathing are my two best pieces of advice on how to adapt successfully within the confines of driver training. Our teens are inundated with a lot of information on a regular basis. Learning to drive requires them to take in even more information about the rules of the road in order to pass the permit and license tests. The rest of the work is muscle memory and no amount of talking will form that base, only behind the wheel practice counts. So, allow your teen to practice in a calm space within the car as I promise that will bring out the sense of most control for everyone. It is fair to point out helpful tips but try, try, try to remember that shouting out comments and reactions to near misses just heightens nervousness and undermines the situation. I venture to say the vast majority of those comments are not going to prevent any accident from occurring. An accident is just that, an accident. We all probably have at least one behind-the-wheel story to share that involves some frustrating incident. We adapt by honoring the fact that the most important aspect of driving is safety, no matter where circumstances lead us. Through adaptation we send the message to our teens that they are our most cherished commodities—not our cars. Our material possessions can be replaced but our kids should always feel they matter most. As I said before, if it's not in you to go through this process with your teen then hire a professional who has a car as part of the package and keep the peace. Or call on a trusted friend, mentor, or relative to guide the instruction along the way. If it is you who will take on the task then bite your tongue, sit back, and let the adventure begin!

ROAD MAPS

I've said it already but I will say it once more: "Bite your tongue." Let your kids determine the timing of when to get a permit and license to drive if there is no necessary time frame. Let a trained professional do the work if you are not up to the task. Adapt with the process to foster independence that will extend to other areas in life. Ultimately, enjoy the ride!

Curfew

Curfew seems to be a topic of contention among parents and teenagers. A lot of issues surface for parents when establishing a set curfew for kids because it seems every family has a different take on what is an acceptable curfew. A common push back from teens on curfew is that friends are allowed to stay out later and your own kids don't want to miss out on anything fun and exciting. No teen ever wants to stand apart from the group and parents are often to blame. I have always found that it is beneficial to be the blame as a parent because it takes the pressure off our kids. I tell my kids all the time to use me as the reason why they have to say no, leave early, not attend something, etc., because it makes them look like they don't want to make the choice but they have no other option. If as a parent you spin it the right way, it takes the pressure off the child of being the bad guy and any criticism from peers can simply be a result of the fact that you are a nasty, unsympathetic parent who just doesn't get it. I am telling you right now that it is absolutely okay to be that kind of parent in the eyes of the peers of your kids. In the long run your kids will find the relief they need by using you as the scapegoat and they may begin to make those choices to use us as the excuse on their own when they realize that it can be effective.

As far as establishing a set curfew for my teens, I have used a similar process for each in the sense that I use legal curfew as my time limit. In our town the legal curfew for a minor is 11:00 p.m. In the city of San Diego it is 10:00 p.m. In the state of California it varies from city to city but the legal curfew is generally 10:00 p.m. or 11:00 p.m. This is the perfect way to take the pressure off you as a parent and simply state that your curfew rules are set by the law. During the preteen years most kids will be home well before 10:00 p.m. unless they are out with you, another parent, or are at a friend's house for a sleepover. Once teens start to venture out on their own, unless they can drive, you determine when and where they will be picked up or coordinate those details with other trusted parents so it's not an issue. When curfew gets tricky is when teens can drive or go off on their own, in which case communication and set rules with time become key.

Curfew is an area where repetition is never overkill. It is important to reiterate boundaries and verbalize curfew times prior to your teen heading out for an activity. Also, by using legal curfews as the limit there is never any gray area, so teens cannot say they were not clear on when they were supposed to be home. Another way to work with your teen on acceptable curfew times is to remind them that curfew is a privilege and if the boundaries are repeatedly honored then it may make sense for later times or special circumstances to be granted. This has been the case with my kids, especially with special circumstances and in the case of my college students, relaxed times when returning home for vacations and summer. Work with your kids within an ongoing framework of trust being the guide.

Curfew for teens can seem like a continuous battle with parents. In many cases it seems parents just don't get the importance of freedom and not missing out on the action. Oftentimes the situation surrounding the boundary of curfew becomes a back and forth point of contention that takes place each time an activity requires a curfew. A time limit is generally set directly by the parent. When the time limit approaches, the idea may be that the teen asks the parent for fifteen more minutes, or a half an hour longer, or explain circumstances that are out of the control of the teen and are causing a delay in the arrival home. This type of back and forth prevents the building of trust. The parent usually says no to the extra time, then bartering begins, or the response to no leeway is ignored, or excuses manifest. This is an exhausting an ineffective approach and should be avoided because the consequence will be no change in curfew and restriction of outings in the future.

Teens most often do not understand the big deal about curfew and are left with a one-way feeling of unreasonable control imposed by the parent. The only reality for the teen is the present world. Curfew breaks the scene, which is the most important place for the teen to be at that time. No one ever wants to be the first one to leave the fun or simply to just stand out. What happens away from the home is the space where the teen is in control and many aspects of socialization take place. This is important and a normal part of the process of maturity, autonomy, and development. The flip side is that the world is not as small and safe as it seems in the confines of the fun. Curfew is best observed as a reasonable guide for socialization, safety, and balance.

Sometimes leaving in the middle of the excitement is the freshest approach. It establishes confidence, control, and prudence and such traits are to be admired. Gratification and self-respect showcase when you don't have to remain part of a whole until the bitter end. It promotes balance and self-awareness. It also leaves room for more fun to stay engaged in subsequent events. If every time a social event takes place and you are there until the bitter end, there may form a feeling of monotony or even a letdown. It may also be that control is lost altogether and unpleasant consequences override initial enjoyment because less consciously grounded choices manifest when going with the flow of peers. Or complete irresponsibility and disaster may end the pleasantness because no boundaries, filters, or limits were practiced. It is through a managed, sensible framework that ultimate enjoyment can be repeatedly experienced. When the curfew rule is maintained it builds relationship, character, and paves the way for getting the most out of time spent.

One aspect of curfew that was great and unique for me while raising my young adults was the fact that we live in a town where it was very easy to walk and ride bikes to get around everywhere instead of having to commute by car. Until my kids reached high school I would estimate that 85 percent of their connection to friends and activities took place in our town. I used legal curfew, 11:00 p.m., as my initial guide when they were off on foot or biked with friends locally. This was a great way for me to build trust around the limits. If they were disciplined enough to maintain consistency in honoring the rule then they were rarely restricted from participating in all of their desired requests to go out. Along with respecting curfew boundaries they were expected to check in periodically to let me know they were okay, usually every two hours, and always when they changed locations. They were also expected to respond if I reached out by call or text to them for some reason. I was fortunate with all three of my kids that they honored the boundaries well early on. We had the initial tug of war with the requests for just a little more time or unforeseen circumstances but through dialog, consideration, and minor consequences the boundaries were maintained with consistency and respect.

One area where we did clearly draw lines was in making sure we personally knew who was in charge when they were going out to other friend's homes. Another big restriction was in limiting premature participation in unsupervised, "popular" parties and any sketchy, vague gatherings where parties might transpire. We took a lot of flak for this initially but in the long run all of our kids recognized the wisdom—especially when they would hear about all of the aftermath in the days to follow. Since trust was built with all of them through communication and respect all of my curfew stories are surrounded by special circumstances. In the course of following the family rules and honoring guidelines each of my teens were given the opportunity to set special limits for various events of importance.

Sam was the first to experience this privilege by his own request and my other two kids followed his lead. For both of his proms (junior and senior) and for his high school graduation he asked for a 4:00 a.m. curfew and we gave it to him. It was an earned "gift" in all cases and by communicating clear details of why he wanted the time and what his plans were going to be, we allowed the space. He was dating a girl, and still is as I write this, and we know her family well. They were going to be at her home after the special event, the fast food run, and their general group of friends disbanded. It was mostly for enjoying the memorable moments as long as possible and then being able to say that such a generous curfew was allowed.

This was the case for a few Fourth of Julys as well, because the Fourth is such a big, big deal in our little hometown. Activities begin at 4:30 a.m. to save spots for the parade route and then take place one after the other all through the day and evening. The saving grace on us as parents is that everything occurs within the confines of our town and most people are on foot or bike. As I said before, in all these special events and with curfew in general we have been very lucky as parents to rarely worry about push back or unpleasant consequences with our kids. There was a circumstance where too much freedom got the best of Sam on the Fourth of July after his first year of college. He and a small group of friends obtained a stash of alcohol and started drinking very early in the day. We received a call from his best friend in the early afternoon, letting us know that

Sam was not doing well, and that we should come and pick him up. When I drove to get him from his friend's care, I arrived to pick up a very drunk boy. He seemed typically drunk and I was not too concerned for his physical safety once I had him with me. I mostly worried that he was going to throw up in my car and then I watched him closely at home as he drank sips of Gatorade and then "passed out" on his bed for several hours.

Ironically, he was allowed to go out and watch the fireworks with his girlfriend later that night. The reason for this was because we had a very open conversation about everything that happened. The conversation took place first with him and then with him and his girlfriend together. I also had a conversation with his best friend about the sequence of events. I learned that at the party where I had to gone to pick him up, which was the home of one of my friends, he had thrown up in their side yard and in a trash can. We talked about how and where he obtained the alcohol. He revealed that he didn't eat a very substantial breakfast and started drinking beer in the morning during the parade. When he arrived at the party after the parade he was already buzzed and he continued to drink because of being surrounded by people handing him alcohol and the momentum of holiday energy. Before he knew it he was completely drunk. When I got him home he was pretty out of it and he slept for a few hours on his bed.

His girlfriend was in a similar position but did not get as sick. I told him he needed to address the social etiquette immediately with the friends at whose home he got sick. He called to ask if there was anything he could do that day to help clean up but he was only able to leave a message and did not hear back. As an immediate conse-quence he had to deal with his hangover and to follow up with our friend, where he was sent to apologize in person the next day. He was allowed to go out to the fireworks because I knew that he would not be drinking, he showed sincere remorse, followed through with his calls and apologies, and became a clear example to his siblings of what not to do on a holiday—or any day for that matter. He went off to the fireworks and then returned home after the finish where he stayed for the remainder of the evening. The following Fourth of July we talked openly about some of the poor choices he made the year prior and he redeemed himself with no repeat performance.

There was a circumstance where my daughter, Sarah, was able to participate in a local party for New Year's Eve. She is very consistent about standing firm in her convictions and though she did not want to go out and drink she did want to be part of the group with her friends who were going out all together to a party where they would hang out to ring in the new year. She was a sophomore in high school and she was friends with a group of girls whom she had been hanging out with since middle school. They were all going to have dinner at the home of our friends and then they were going to stay together as a group and head to a party of some people in town who we knew, yet only as acquaintances. The parents were to be present the entire time at the home, so we figured everything would be well regulated.

My daughter checked in periodically during the course of the evening to let us know she was doing fine. She and another one of her girlfriends made a pact with each other that they were going to avoid alcohol consumption altogether. The rest of the group they were with did not make the same decision. It turns out the parents hosting the party did not either. We found out after the fact that they were in a completely different part of the house the entire evening with a group of their own friends. There was a designated room that night in their home that was specifically being used for drugs. There were kids playing drinking games with hard liquor and before my daughter knew it she was surrounded by drunk kids everywhere doing stupid and crazy things with each other and with alcohol.

The cops were called to break up the party and just before they arrived one of my daughter's friends appeared and she could barely stand up on her own. Sarah spent the rest of her night making sure the girl was okay by staying with her and keeping her upright and safe until her parents arrived. She was assisting several other friends as well, with her other friend who was also completely sober. As all the kids scattered, fled, and stumbled to wherever they could to get away when the party was being broken up, my daughter was questioned by police, who very quickly realized she was sober and thanked her for her assistance in standing by and helping to contact parents for friends. It was a crazy night for her, with a much different outcome from my son's Fourth of July. It made my daughter realize that she did not want to go to any more parties, even just to hang out. She did not have fun, did not like being around drunk people, witnessed a lot of inappropriate physical conduct, and never once saw the parents intervene responsibly.

Due to the fact that she was insistent about maintaining her boundaries, and asked probing questions about why the group of friends continued to make choices—even after that party—to place themselves in situations where it was too easy to fall into the same pattern, she was excluded from the group. Her best friend at the time, the girl who she literally held up that night, stopped talking with her altogether with no heads-up or explanation. My daughter was bullied, ostracized, and cast aside by her girlfriends and boyfriends alike. She started two and a half years of unanticipated solitude from "best" friends and graduated high school with no girlfriends from her own class. As far as my daughter's curfew is concerned it has never really been an issue. It has consistently been 11:00 p.m. due to legal curfew and she was given special circumstance with time for New Year's Eve, the Fourth of July, and a handful of school dances.

Both of the stories shared above highlight examples of my kids being able to set a later curfew for a special circumstance because they earned the privilege. For both kids the outcome of the events was not that great, even though they both probably anticipated that not having an early curfew was going to make the evening such a blast. We tend to place a lot of emphasis on special circumstances. It may be just as important for teens to realize there can be some letdown when anticipation is high as it is for them to experience the great feeling about the fact that they earned a benefit for their conscious behavior. The application of MAPS in the scenario of curfew teaches rights, consequences, choices, and actions. A lot of the lessons to everyone in the stories came solely from repercussions of behavior when given freedom. My teens learned valuable lessons because we broke down the event through straightforward, factual dialogue, not judgment. They were able to internalize the necessary ramifications of their actions while letting go of the details that no longer served a purpose.

In the case of Sam, he knew he made a poor choice and he felt lousy about it, had to deal with his hangover, an apology to several people, and a semi-ruined fun day because of the hours his drinking took away. There would have been no added benefit in restricting him from going to the fireworks; he had learned his lesson and I didn't need to top it with anger toward me that would not have had any direct correlation to him not making the choice again in the future. By standing for the principles of MAPS, I modeled for him how I would have wanted the situation to be handled if I were my own parent. He learned a tough lesson because his own behaviors taught him much of the lesson, we maintained open communication, and he realized that even without me chastising him directly he would have to work a little harder next time to maintain trust and respect.

In the case of Sarah, she learned a very difficult lesson while doing everything right. In the case of MAPS, I started to participate with her in many of the things good friends do together and for one another while modeling my boundaries as a parent overall. She needed reinforcement and connection while Sam needed me to slow down and be present for his care and aftermath. My best advice for setting curfew with your teens is to model and slow down. The best application of MAPS on this topic is to slow down. Connect with your teen on the details of what they are trying to accomplish in staying out late. Communicate with your teen about the consequences of staying out late and the risks involved in circumstances attached to it. Nothing really great happens after 11:00 p.m. for the most part. This is generally when people get sloppy, try to get away with bad behavior, drive drunk, prowl around, sneak, hide, break rules, etc. I know these actions are stereotypical in a sense but it's relatively true that such things happen more frequently in the later hours of the night. There is no reason for your teen to be out after legal curfew and minimizing risk and exposure is part of the premise behind having the law in the first place. Have a conversation with your teen about what kind of things they are going to be doing after curfew that they think are going to be so fun they don't want to miss out. Chances are they have had plenty of time prior to their curfew to participate in the excitement. Anything happening after curfew is probably unnecessary or something that you don't want them to be doing anyway. If they want to push the curfew line then invite the group of friends over to your own home and have a sleepover or have everyone plan to leave at the time of a group set curfew hour.

The other important side of having a curfew and the concept of slowing down is to get enough required sleep for teens as they grow and develop. This might sound like a silly reason but there are plenty of studies that can be accessed and shared supporting the critical importance of sleep for teens. It's a two-way street in the sense that a curfew sets up respect for the rest parents need as well. Wake up for your teen coming home to meet curfew and check in face-to-face on their safe return. Have a quick conversation about the details of the night and then see them to bed. This way accountability is established, you know they are safe, and you know they are healthy. Then, hold yourself to the same standard of slowing down.

I realized that I used to go out with friends quite frequently as a coping mechanism for the dysfunction of my marriage. My kids always saw me leaving the house and wouldn't see me return before their bedtime. Once I recognized the pattern, I needed to learn how to model choices for slowing down, and really be present for the details of their social needs and desires. My sixteen-year-old son, Shaun, who is now the only one at home with me, just commented to me how he told his friends, a newer group that he has been hanging out with from his school, that he tells me everything. They were impressed and I felt so honored and thankful that he was proud to mention such a fact. I am also very thankful that such open communication takes place between me and my kids on a regular basis because I do try to slow down and make myself available.

The choice to slow down is a simple one. It may not always be easy, and it often involves retraining and some finesse, but for the most part your friends, work, and obligations will just start to realize that your kids are a priority. Time slips quickly away so make the most of the moments you have with them now. Motivate them to understand that your curfew is valid just as your relationship with them is valid. Slowing down enables respect to override all the seemingly negative aspects of imposing curfew because it puts relationship and care above restriction.

ROAD MAPS

Eliminate gray area and use legal curfew as a guide to set rules. Be consistent about sticking with legal parameters to avoid a tug-of-war over extra time out. Allow kids to earn privileges for special circumstances by following curfew consistently so they are motivated to respect the rules on a regular basis. Communicate any change in location, every time it happens, for safety reasons. Reciprocate the rules for your teens when you are out or away. Model expected behavior by slowing down and showing up when your kids need you—just like you are asking them to do for you.

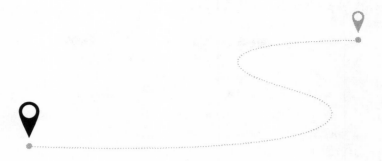

School and Homework

School and homework are two things most kids have to deal with on a regular basis as they grow from infancy into young adulthood. As parents, most of us remember the day in and day out grind of school and homework from our own childhood. Though both are generally unavoidable, as parents today we have more options for how to school our children and the impact of homework as part of the process. The choices may include public schools, private schools, charter schools, development academies, vocational schools, creative schools, online schools, boarding schools, and home schools to name a few. On top of that are multiple preschool and day care philosophies to consider before "required" schooling even begins. Some preschools even have a waiting list that infants can be put on as soon as they are born in order to secure a spot by the time they reach the age of three. I can wholeheartedly admit that I was a little over the top when it came to making decisions about schools for my firstborn. I wanted the perfect everything when it came to making the very first choices. Like most choices we make as parents for our kids, we realize, through time and experience, that there is always a "Plan B" when the best choice fails to be the ultimate. We may form a more relaxed ideology about the necessity of perfect choices with each successive child and that is great in the sense that there are no cookie-cutter solutions. It's important to remember that each child is different, therefore different options and considerations are completely appropriate.

As children, school can be exciting, overwhelming, fun, tedious, interesting, boring, stressful, safe, suppressive, social, engaging, eye-opening, or all of the above depending on the day! So many unique scenarios and happenings play out each day with school that shape character and develop the mind through the foray of a learning environment. The process can also play out very differently from year to year due to various factors. Teachers, administrators, classmates, campuses, rooms, subjects, teaching styles, rules, schedules, and the like all impact and shape through exposure. School is a major part of the formative years in the life of many kids. Adding homework to the mix forms another layer to the school experience that can vary widely from person to person and through environment. There can often be a sense of pressure to excel in school and with homework that go hand in hand. The pressure can be internally formed, externally expected, or a little of both. Measure and comparison are frequently exercised in school and with homework as a matter of qualifying what is being taught. The problem is that sometimes it can feel like an interpretation of worth when it is not at all. In basic form, school is really just a means to an end when it comes to socialization and academic contribution to society. It is really nothing more.

With Sam, I stressed out about making the perfect decision for his schooling from day one. I wanted the environment to be just right so I did a lot of research, signed him up on waiting lists, and continued to formulate a checklist for the best environment to immerse him during his time away from home. The answer came through a communication about a reverse mainstream preschool that was going to be starting at our elementary school. For the inaugural year they would take four preschool-age, mainstream students within a section of the special needs class. The concept was to teach tolerance, basic skills, and routines in an all-inclusive school setting. I was thrilled by the sense of compassion, the credentials of the teacher, the school setting, and the unique environment for Sam. He was accepted to the program as one of the four mainstream students and he had an amazing year. We were all set to send him to year two with the program, as a four-year-old, and found out only a few weeks before the start of school that the teacher was leaving due to a mismatch in philosophy with administration and the program was no longer going to be available.

Needless to say, this put us completely behind with timing, space, and options when it came to making a "Plan B" decision. The preschool I wanted him to attend as a first choice outside of his other program was full to capacity and had a huge waitlist even if a spot did become available. The local choice we ended up making was a Montessori school, with a great ideology that seemed like it would be a great fit. We learned within the first few weeks that it was not the right choice for Sam at all, for a number of different reasons. The school did not match his personality, but the clincher came through a stranger danger talk, given by an outside organization, that scared my son to the point of tears and prevented us from being able to drop him and leave after several attempts across multiple days that followed. Due to the fact that I was a stay-at-home mom, I quickly came to the conclusion that preschool was not necessary for him that year.

Although the scenario seemed to be disastrous at first, it really did help make all the other decisions about preschool so much easier as our other kids started. It took the pressure off too, when I realized that preschool was not essential for our family. My daughter, Sarah, had a great experience for both of her preschool years in a local school where I met most of the female friends I still have to this day. My son Shaun was not ready for preschool when he first started at three so, after a few weeks of trying with no change in tears or homesickness, we pulled him out. Seven months later, while out walking Shaun in his stroller, we passed by the front of the preschool and he announced to me, "That is my school!" I said he was right and asked if he wanted to go there now. I called the school that day, found a spot in a different class than he originally started for his age group, took him to school that next day, and he loved it. He attended preschool that year from March until May and then he began preschool the following year with the same teacher as a four-year-old and finished out the entire year with success and fun.

All three of my kids attended public, local elementary and middle school in our hometown. They had fairly standard experiences with good teachers, a mix of friends, and a progression of learning from year to year. In the early years we sat with them during homework time, but as they grew and matured, homework became something that we wanted them to take personal responsibility toward. Not to mention the fact that by middle school they were all taking math and science courses that challenged my own ability to tutor them successfully. They all learned self-motivation and consequence at early ages with homework. I feel strongly that a progressive hands-on to hands-off approach is the best course of action. Our kids learned quickly that homework is a personal responsibility that can have an impact on grades. They also each came up with their own strategies for how best to conquer the task. It's not always easy to find a balance of school and homework when kids are active in extracurricular activities. Each one of the kids played in one or more sports beginning at the age of four. Oftentimes, as they got older, they would practice and play sports requiring a chunk of time to commute. We would work with them to come up with solutions and strategies for how best to conquer all the tasks required in a day. Occasionally that would mean making choices about going or not going to practice, doing or not doing homework, getting or not getting sleep, and developing insight about standing up for themselves and successfully prioritizing and understanding commitments. A lot of character building takes place through adaptation when learning to trust inner voices on how to measure and balance priorities.

When it came time to make a choice about where to attend high school for Sam, I stressed myself out to try and make the perfect decision once again. I had in the back of my mind that I wanted him to attend a private, all-boy Catholic high school instead of the local high school within walking distance of our home. I began planting seeds starting in middle school. Each year of middle school, I would mention at the beginning and end of the year, my desire for him to think about attending Saint Augustine High School. Every time I broached the subject with him and/or his father, I was met with resistance. When it came time to actually consider the choice as an option I pushed a little harder.

My son wanted to know why I thought it would be a good idea for him to go to such a school. I explained to him that the main reason was because I liked the idea of an all-boy environment encompassing families from across the county, not just from our town. He had no strong friend group in his grade. I was worried that his shyness and amiability may connect him with a group not well suited to his best interests. He might take a go-with-the-flow mentality in a crowd not held to the same morals and values we were trying to impart as a family. The idea of a school designed to teach, mentor, shape, and hold accountable all boys would give him every opportunity to thrive. He would be held to no-tolerance standards, taught manners, timeliness, camaraderie, and brotherhood with the same philosophy of spiritual beliefs as our family and the ability to talk openly about faith. It would be his place and I wanted him to be exposed to as many healthy, varied role models as possible. It felt like a winning situation to me all the way around. I told him we were giving him a choice and an opportunity. If he went through the process of applying to the school, he would have nothing to lose. It would open a new environment of possibility for him. If he were to be accepted then a choice could be made. If he didn't go through the process then no choice would present.

He agreed to go through the steps for me. His father agreed to let him go through the steps as well. Before he knew that he was accepted to the school, my son came to me and told me that he really wanted to go to the school. He made it in and accepted the spot. In his four years at Saint Augustine High School he grew into more of a quality young man than I could ever hope. He endured many of the same trials he may have in our local school, with searching for friend groups, finding a spot on the sports teams, ups and downs with girls, and the like. What stood out above any opportunities locally were the development of a strong faith, a brotherhood, the ability to be taught with movement, critical thinking, uninhibited male energy, no-tolerance policies for moral and social development, timeliness, respect for a rule of life, sports championships, and ultimately a specific, Augustinian, full-tuition scholarship to his college. He also paved the way for the choice to be presented to his younger brother when it was time for him to attend high school. Shaun made the same choice and continues to have similar and personal blessings.

When it came time to make the choice for my daughter to attend high school locally, or elsewhere in the county, we tried a similar approach. What we found was that there was no equivalent school to Saint Augustine for girls. There is an all-girl, Catholic high school for girls in San Diego County, but it was not the right environment for my daughter. I must also admit that I have a double standard when it comes to single-sex high schools. I do not believe that an all-girl environment is beneficial for girls in the same way an all-boy environment is beneficial for boys. It is kind of like the Girl Scouts and Boy Scouts to me. For certain reasons I find more benefit to boys in both cases. It's not necessary for me to go into the reasons other than to highlight that we gave my daughter that same choice as her brothers to stay locally or go elsewhere. With her options, which were the local high school, a coed Catholic high school, or an all-girl high school, she chose the local high school. Her choice was the best for her, and although it was extremely challenging socially, it also turned out that she landed a full-tuition scholarship to her first-choice college. This was due to academics, financial need, and merit.

My point in sharing all three stories of my kid's high school choices is to support that one size does not fit all. Adapt. Open worlds for your kids even if they don't initially think it is what they want. Teach them how to look at pros and cons. Make informed decisions. Always offer choices where you can. Share personal stories about your own school years and experiences. No situation is ever perfect but as parents we have insight into our kids that enable us to see things that they might otherwise miss out on. The concept of MAPS encourages branching out. There is often more than one way to get to the same place, so find the road that is best. If, as a parent, you see a path before your kids recognize one, introduce it. Modeling the conversation puts it on the table. Adapting to push back, looking at options, encouraging process, and taking steps open all avenues of possibility. The decision-making process is one that all parties can participate. There are multiple ways for everyone to break down a step-by-step solution to find the best outcome. Never be afraid to take it slow. I did with the high school decisions. Yet, with some of the other school stories, the choices were quick and reactive. They were all thought out, and they were all best choices. It was a lot of finding the right destination and then rerouting when it didn't feel right anymore. If circumstances allow, then find new places as necessary. The ultimate message for this chapter is to do your homework, follow MAPS, and see where it takes you.

ROAD MAPS

All the concepts of MAPS apply to this section so the highlight is to advocate for your child. School and homework can shape potential so use MAPS to guide your kids toward their highest good. When they know that is your hope for them they will learn self-motivation to the same end. The cause and effect nature of school and homework mirror what our teens will be up against out in the greater world. These formative years are a lot like a play about life, so as you move through scenes and work on props together, let your teen set the stage.

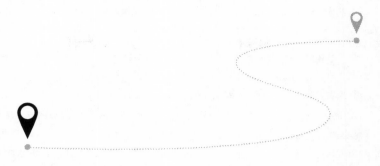

Family

Family is defined simply as parents and children living together in a unit. It sounds simple but it is anything but—especially below the surface. The definition of family constantly evolves. Definition of family can be set by what we project and also by what is assumed. Unless I specify that I am a divorced mom, the notion is that I have a husband when I am talking about my kids in a surface capacity. As a mother in a family that wasn't exactly what it seemed to be on the surface, I understand that the framework of family can speak volumes without words just by public display of the family unit. Through years of church services, camping trips, volunteer efforts, concerts in the park, parties, sports, and vacations everyone in those circles assumed that we were an amazingly wonderful, tight-knit, healthy, happy family. Even those closest to our family, who knew so much more about quiet struggles and discord, assumed that our family was an amazing, unshakable unit.

The image of family is well accepted when all members of the group are consistently visible. It doesn't matter if we hold secrets, trauma, dissatisfaction, dysfunction, disease, and everything in between inside, the perception precedes reality and the expectation of the visible core is that all is well. As grown adults we come from our own families of origin with a learned understanding that no matter how dysfunctional, the function is in playing family. In playing family we function to the best of our ability within the parameters. So, what appears simple and straightforward about family may not always be the case. Make it as simple as possible by slowing down, being present and offering your best each day. Remember that each individual within the family is unique and plays a part.

As children, the family of origin is what is familiar and "normal." Kids believe for the longest time that all families function the same way as theirs. It is not until they become a little older and begin to spend time at friends' and relatives' homes that they realize other people may do things completely differently. The insight can be comforting or it can be disconcerting. The same is true in relation to the parents, too. I remember my kids coming home from sleepovers or vacations with other families and remarking on how much they yell, disrespect one another, and glorify different values. I also remember conversations when my kids would question why I couldn't be more like other parents in my attitude and perspective on specific topics. The famous and frequent comment was that I was the only parent with such strict, conservative rules. It is important for kids to relate with peers on issues when it comes to family. Most kids do not want their family to stand out in any negative or restrictive way. Kids want to be able to say yes to everything, fit in seamlessly, and be accepted on every level. The family framework can have a way of challenging the comfortable world in which our children would love to live all of the time.

It seems to me that family often takes a back seat to all of the schedules, activities, work, school, friends, and access to all that we have at our fingertips in this day and age. My mantra for families is a resounding "Slow down!" It is important to realize this as soon as possible and set some time aside for family only. The good news is that family time habits can be adopted at any point. Instituting family habits as kids become older may require a little more effort but it is well worth the energy. The easiest way to establish set family time is to schedule at least one meal a day together. If it cannot be dinner, then make it breakfast. If it cannot be scheduled with the entire family during the week, have a set mealtime when the majority of family members can be present and schedule whole family meals on the weekends. Family dinner is the greatest time to bond without seeming as though bonding is taking place and it is an open forum for discussion for anything and everything. It has become a running joke with my kids and their friends, now that they are older, that our family discussions are the most fun, funny, and uncensored conversations around.

We began using dinnertime as a place to check in with everyone. We would ask about closest moments to God, one funny thing that stood out in the day, or open up with questions, concerns, and town news. We got in the habit of discussing drugs if it was Red Ribbon Week at school, or alcohol if the kids knew of parties taking place that night. I would bring up stories/news that I learned about my kids' peers so they would begin to understand that I would always find out what was going on whether they wanted me to or not. I would also share stories about myself, my friends, relatives, etc., so they would begin to understand, relate, and feel a part of community. Family meal discussions are also a great way to establish respect with one another through listening, encouragement, connection, and trust. There were many times we would discuss topics such as politics, local "gossip," finances, prayer requests, and morals, which would require keeping confidences. Learning how to honor a confidence builds respect and trust among family members and promotes the home as a safe haven. If it is absolutely impossible to have family mealtime on a regular basis, establish a family game night or movie night once a week. We would schedule one weekend night for either or and sometimes it would feel forced, but it always ended well once enacted.

Another aspect of family I would reinforce regularly was that life among siblings and family members is never equal but always fair. The general statement from me was that what comes around eventually goes around. This is an especially big deal in families with more than one child. When it comes to rules, gifts, opportunities, and the like it seems that kids really want everything to be equal. Trying to strive for equality in such matters is a losing battle in my eyes, and rarely mimics the way life actually works. I do believe it is important to understand and support the idea of appropriateness in relation to equality. My take on it with the kids was just what I stated above . . . in time, most everything balances out. Also, different kids often have different needs, so I made a habit of explaining the differences due to birth order, gender, and circumstances to name a few. I would often share stories of my own upbringing, which would reveal the pitfalls of striving for equality and showcase examples of future results managing to rectify seeming inequities in some capacity.

A clear example from our own family that still stands out to this day but highlights the concept in an acceptable way for all members has to do with cell phones. It was a family rule that our kids would not receive cell phones until ninth grade—the start of high school—and would not get texting privileges until the beginning of tenth grade. Such a rule seems almost barbaric in this day and age and none of our kids were happy at the time for such restriction. The philosophy behind the rule was that we live in a town where cell phones are not a necessity for many different reasons. Our kids were not attending activities or school out of town before high school without us. They would ride bikes back and forth the distance of ten blocks to school. All of their friends were in town. Sports practice was a bike ride or a local carpool away. My parents, my sister and her family, my cousin and her family, and my aunt and uncle all live within blocks of one another and the school, so if there was ever an emergency and I was not on the island for some reason, there were plenty of sufficient and safe backup resources. We also felt very strongly, and still do, as parents who grew up in a different generation, that cell phones are stunting articulate, genuine levels of communication development in today's youth. We wanted all of our kids to learn how to successfully communicate with us, each other, and friends without cell phones impeding the process. We also wanted to know the friends that our kids were hanging out with, so using our own cell phone to set up social time enabled the open exchange for everyone. It really didn't impede too much of what our children were doing at all, but it greatly benefited them in other ways.

Not having a cell phone before freshman year of high school taught them more conscious self-awareness habits and promoted tangible effort in communicating with us when we asked. Having a cell phone was for emergencies only and for a means of direct contact when we required taught responsibility and accountability before extending texting privileges. Offering texting later did require that they finesse oral conversations as a precursor to written "talk." We watched all this work and believed that what we were doing was the best choice for our kids. We even managed Sam's relationship with his girlfriend in eighth and ninth grade—when she moved off the island before she began high school—without a cell phone initially. We knew the family, would drive him back and forth, knew where he was, and were thankful that he had to call and talk to her on his cell phone in high school instead of just texting all the time. There were apps that they would use to text without cell phone texting but texting was not always available as a primary means of communication.

The change in perspective on the rule came when our youngest son, Shaun, was in middle school. He took up skateboarding as a regular activity with his friends. They would skateboard in the front of the house, around town, and at the local skate park. All seemed well until one day he fell at the skate park and hurt himself to the point of needing medical attention. The chain of communication was inhibited because he didn't have immediate access to a phone. He had to alert his friend, who's cell phone wasn't charged, so another phone needed to be used and that phone didn't have any of our numbers in it, then we didn't recognize the number, multiple people were called and there was a breakdown in who was on the way to help him and it turned into a big mess. There were also times when he would head to the skate park alone, in which case the breakdown would've been much less effective on top of all the other issues. We started to realize by the end of the summer that it made sense for him to have a cell phone for emergency use if he was going to be skateboarding regularly.

So, in August, for his thirteenth birthday, just before the start of his eighth grade school year, we gave him a basic cell phone as one of his surprise gifts. We took him out to a birthday dinner at a place of his choosing with our whole family, as our usual tradition. When he opened his new cell phone he was so excited and our other two kids became openly angered. It took us aback a little as we explained our reasoning, but both older kids remained adamant that it was completely unfair and that he was so spoiled as the youngest child. They stayed angry over the circumstances for some time but now they completely understand my regular comment that life is not always equal but usually always fair in one way or another. They have had other occurrences happen with travel, cars, phones, relationships, and situations where they have experienced firsthand, each child in a separate way, the sensibility of my perspective and how life begins to work in various ways at various times. Today we can all talk about that standout situation with a laugh.

It is also interesting to note that my daughter was recently asked to speak to a group of mothers and daughters attending a "coming of age" seminar. She is known in some circles of our community as a role model for prudence, chastity, and modesty in her actions and character. One of the question and answer topics focused on cell phones and my daughter explained to a large group of girls and moms our family rule on cell phones, and stated that she was thankful now for our decisions. She was able to communicate to all of them the benefits of our choices for her at this point in her life and she expressed thanks for the philosophy and mandate. She came home and shared with me that she now understands and appreciates our choices in respect to our cell phone decisions. She can see the fruits and can say in hindsight that she gets our decisions. It was such a blessing and a confirmation to me that our reasoning resounded with her in such a healthy, distinct way.

It is easy to envision that so many of the issues surrounding family can be best served with all of concepts of MAPS. My best tip for family life in general is to instill habits of ways to slow down. To parent well it is mandatory to model behavior if we want to watch our kids mirror expected habits. It is also important to participate when it comes to family for the same reasons we need to model. It is one thing to verbalize expectations but quite another to actively engage, for and with our children. It also makes sense to say that the decision to give our youngest son a cell phone an entire year sooner than our family rule was because we needed to adapt, and that is a fact.

Yet, the overarching theme of success when it comes to family dynamics is rooted in the practice of learning to slow down. When we slow down as families we gain perspective on the essence of connection. Value as members of a working unit can be applied in so many ways when we stop and savor each other, ideas, time, and energy to face each day to the best of our ability. Slow down and spend time with one another. Slow down and engage. Instead of plunging continuously through lists of responsibilities give them a momentary back seat. Slow down and evaluate rhythms and routines.

Slow down and witness. Slow down and pay attention. Do not ignore what is right in front of you. Family can be very easy to take for granted because in a way we are stuck with one another for better or for worse. So, make the best of who you are and what you have by being present. Presence requires pause and pause means we have to stop for a moment. If we don't learn how to stop then we haven't accepted the process of slowing down and we all know too well that means that life will continue to just quickly pass us by. Capture precious moments through the nature of slowing down and I promise you will benefit from the gifts of slow that manifest into go because slow will create the bond that helps make go all the better.

ROAD MAPS

Accept that your family is your family and give thanks where you can. Grow for the better whenever possible by focusing on modeling desired behavior. Grow from one another by slowing down. Plan a daily mealtime where everyone sits and eats at the same time. Build in family "down" time with movie night, game night, pizza night, or something that involves a change from going out or separate activities. All of the concepts of MAPS work for family because there are so many different aspects. Try not to take each other for granted. There are ways to highlight and compliment unique traits from each member. The focus should be on fairness through the scheme of life. Don't anticipate that every situation is going to be equal. Connect and communicate with one another to add value as a whole.

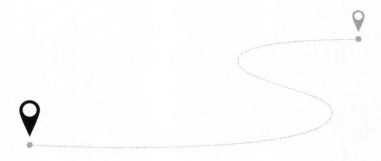

Friends

The topic of kids and friends is ever changing. One of the most important areas in raising kids is to strike the right balance between control and autonomy with friends. When our kids are little, we have it easy as parents because we control who our kids spend time with one hundred percent of the time, with few exceptions. As our kids get older, we lose a little control over who they interact with as friends due to socialization at school, extracurricular activities, and more developed personal preference. When they reach the teen years there can be outright battles over who we allow our kids to spend time with as friends and oftentimes we lose the battle because of how easy it is to interact with whomever they choose through social media. On top of social media access, teens are much more creative at finding ways around boundaries if we do not address a healthy parenting style around friend choices early on.

Teenagers want friends to be whomever they please, whenever they choose. In the early years friends are generally made through parent's friend's kids, playdates, and interactions through extracurricular activities and school. Growing up imposes awkward choices of how to hang around or not with parent's friend's kids. Issues can arise

with socialization hierarchies, conflicting personalities, and development of different interests with other friends that worked when kids
were younger and become strained as preteens. Teenagers may not
want to hang out with parents at all, let alone parent's friend's kids.
So, a battle for power and opinion over friend choices can become
common. Social standing can also play a big role in who teens want
as friends and why. Fitting in is big motivation for seeking out friends,
and the kids who are the most desirable from a teen perspective
can often be the worst choice. Even so, one of the least desirable
outcomes surrounding who to hang out with and why is having a
parent impose restrictions for no good reason. Often, a ban to keep
company with a friend has the opposite affect by enticing preference
even when knowing the choice is a bad one. Once the cycle starts
it is a slippery slope with unpredictable outcomes.

Sam became friends with a boy who had a bit of a reputa-
tion through town that preceded him. It was nothing that I felt was
warranted or even tangible for that matter, as small towns can have
a way of generating exaggerated opinion. Many times the person
communicating information is not even directly connected to the
elevated gossip. When Sam first started setting up time with friends,
independent of direct supervision, my requirements were that I meet
at least one of the parents and that I meet the friend in person. I also
required a contact number for the parent, friend, or both. The course
of the friendship was then mostly left to my kids. I usually (actually
never thus far) do not step in the middle of a friendship, even if
something goes wrong that requires conflict resolution. My kids are
responsible for participating in the friendship, following house rules,
maintaining boundaries, accepting consequences, and fostering
relationships. I am available for support, loyalty, insight, perspective,
and feedback.

In the case of my son and his friend, there was no reason for me
to mistrust or impose restriction for any reason when they started

hanging out. I monitor and observe from my own position and what I noticed from the start between them was that each brought out the best in the other. They are both still friends, and that statement is still the case. It is not that the friendship has been without incident, but they handle it on their level and still ultimately have the other's back. There are funny, crazy stories throughout about mishaps, misunderstandings, and misgivings but the bottom line is that we are all invested in the connection due to our continued care for one another.

My daughter had a much different experience in the beginning of her teen years that turned out to be not at all what was anticipated in the end. She became friends with a couple different groups of girls and formed close friendships with a few—two of whom I felt she would be good friends with through the years. The initial connection was school and sports that allowed for daily continuity. Sarah was so close with one of the girls that when she learned that her father and I were getting a divorce she called her friend before anyone else to share her heartbreak and find comfort and support in the way she needed it most. My daughter's other friend relied on her as a first line of similar support with boys, parties, questions, conscience, etc. In both cases I was also friends with the moms of the girls. We all spent a lot of time together at games, driving, social school events, and the like.

In both cases there was a swift transition from support, honesty, and openness to exclusion and complete disrespect of my daughter as a caring and kind individual. It is true on one level that my daughter is uncompromising in her morals and values but the backlash for holding the line was not only surprising to me but deeply disheartening. Mean girls control by blacklisting, not just from the group but by ostracizing in the general school social population. It's a subtle yet direct play of "power" via manipulation due to insecurities and fear. Girls in general think that they will be handed the same fate if they don't conform and follow the most popular "leader." The result is either to succumb, find new friends, or stand alone.

My hope was that my daughter would seek out new friends but when you feel as though you have done nothing wrong and don't understand why you feel like you don't fit in anywhere anymore it is challenging to consistently venture out. The overwhelming and personal feeling of hurt and the vague potential reach of conspiracy can be consuming in so many ways. I wanted to build up and support my daughter, not force her into possible repeat exclusion. No one wants to watch a child suffer the consequences of rejection from the undue backlash of being a mirror to your peers. I certainly don't know many of the specific details and I suspect that there was a lot more going on behind the scenes in those girls' lives than anyone cared to reveal or admit. I know there has been in our lives.

I chose to be both a mother and a friend to my daughter and in many ways it served us both well. We had an accessible, nonstop companion for all things "girly." She learned how to articulate well and comfortably with my adult female friends. She taught me how to be less judgmental, to focus on the hurts at hand—not my own past—and be more forgiving with myself, her, and others. We still work together and depend on each other in life strengthening, insightful, and honest ways. Unfortunately, she ended her last two years of high school with no girlfriends in her grade. She still endures the ignorance of being mostly disregarded by these "friends" when paths cross unsuspectingly. There is a level of rising above by some of us involved—especially with the mothers. But I must admit that it is still a big challenge for me to be polite and forgiving when I run into the girls. There is a silver lining in the circumstances in that my daughter chose to use the extra time to serve others, and also reach out to dear friends not in her grade or at her school. She still finds it complicated to connect with girls in an authentic way as she searches for meaningful friendships in her out-of-state university. It seems to me that the majority of individuals from the teen years and beyond struggle with authentic exchange. Finding true friends is a quest.

My youngest son, Shaun, has had a mix of both experiences. He has been ostracized, rejected, misunderstood, sought out, built up, teased, accepted, appreciated, and enjoyed by both girls and guys alike. He found a wonderful mix of sincere friends in his hometown and otherwise due to the fact that he now goes to private high school "over the bridge" after attending school in town through eighth grade. He has a small circle of friends in each category that touch his life and he operates in a sensitive, authentic, committed way in all situations that arise through his relationships. I must admit that I don't even know all his friends or their families as well as I managed with my two older kids. I trust his judgment and ethics mixed with the fact that I let go of so much by the time of his turn to experience. He navigates well with a great balance of love and independence. He is no exception to holding a line and standing for his morals, values, and beliefs. I continually communicate expectations with him but let him gently guide me when it comes to his friend choices and social calendar.

The bottom line is that the topic of friends has everything to do with participation when it comes to MAPS. Participate in connection, conversation, and consequence. Guiding friendship choices with your kids has less to do with control and more to do with consensus. Consensus requires active participation and creates quality relationships even when the friend may not seem like the "perfect" choice on the surface. Consensus through participation also creates win-win results within friendships. Honesty and respect are major keys to actively maintain a good relationship. I try to model good friend choices in my own life to show my kids the value in authentic participation. I share stories about why I spend time with certain friends and why I choose to let others go. It is not always because I have the same agenda as who I choose to spend time with either. I communicate the value of my friends in an open exchange of thoughts and ideals and how complimentary or opposing philosophies can actually be best choices in many ways. Participation means we give and get, grow and build, live and love through similarities and differences.

My guiding rule of thumb when it comes to my kids and their friend choices is in what the friend brings out in my child. If my son or daughter is someone I want to emulate and introduce to others when they are in the presence of the friend then I think the choice of friend is a good one. If that is not the case then participate in finding out why. If a few fluky mishaps are mixed in with an overall congenial personality then communicate, support, and respond favorably. If the actions and behavior of your son or daughter are repeatedly less than desirable then communicate, respond, and participate in educating your kids about the consequences of choices and actions with certain types of influencing personalities. Steer them away by participating in conversations, modeling attributes, and scheduling activities that expose more acceptable interactions. Another way to shift "bad" friend choices is to invite the person to hang out in the home as a main option and include the friend when participating in family activities and adventures. This will reveal a lot and may lend to a path for natural separation instead of an enticing restriction. The idea is to engage, not dictate, and allow everyone to come out the better in the long run.

ROAD MAPS

Restricting friend choices with your kids can often bring on opposing desires. Focus on consensus through questions, conversations, and interactions that draw out the authenticity of a friendship. Analyze your own perspective and what may be driving it (don't restrict a friendship simply because you happen to not like the parent for example) as well as your teen's (does the friend choice bring out the best in your child or is it motivated by something else). Participate in exchanges and activities within your own home to determine if the friendship is healthy or otherwise. Or include the friend in family activities to get to know them better. Be a friend to your kids but always remember that your primary role is as a parent.

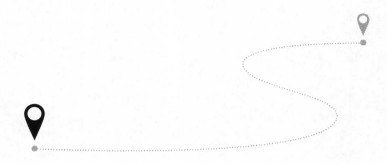

Drugs and Alcohol

The topic of drugs is never an easy one to bring up with kids. As a parent we may think that bringing up the topic will expose our kids to information they are not aware of and that we do not want them to know anyway. What I have found in the course of raising my teens is that any subject we think may be premature is already one that has come up among their friends and schoolmates. The guidelines I try to follow are the ones that the school systems initiate through Red Ribbon Week and similar programs. Thousands of kids under the age of twenty-one die each year due to alcohol abuse. There is a program in the public schools where during the course of an entire school day they make an announcement every set number of minutes that a teen dies due to alcohol. This is the time when we would broach alcohol and drug related discussions in our family. It is easy to bring up the topic when it relates to a school event because it is the perfect forum for educational discussions that have nothing to do with distrust or suspicion on the part of parents to kids. You can bring up the topic in a neutral way, find out how the school is presenting information, and open the discussion to personal and family points of view. It is easy to ask questions and inform your kids about sensitive topics when the basis is neutral.

The topic of drugs can fit into the discussions about alcohol as a drug as well. Our kids are exposed to so many more dangers involving drugs than ever before because there is so much more accessibility and new types of drugs and ways to use them that were not around when we were growing up. It is extremely important to educate kids early due to this fact. I tell my kids all the time that the act of trying a drug even just one time can kill you. With fentanyl and heroin and the capability to lace drugs with either, the danger of death is a fact. With the legalization of marijuana in many states, the topic of drugs is a must. Legal marijuana use is justified on many levels but the fact remains that regular marijuana use under the age of thirty-five permanently impacts normal brain development and negates touted health benefits. Educate yourself and educate your kids! This is not a topic to leave hanging. It's a little like social media in the sense that if you show your kids that you are well informed they will be more inclined to trust and respect you when discussing the topic. Also, it's a great subject to have kids teach you about as well. Find out what they are learning in school, from friends, and who is doing what, when, and where.

I remember being a teen and how important it was to want to fit in with friends socially in every way. I can honestly say that is one thing that has not changed in this day and age. What is different about today than it was when I was growing up is the introduction of social media. It is possible to fit in more readily through social media channels but the flip side is that social media can create a false self and also be very isolating. There is a notion that acceptance comes from the number of followers and/or the number of likes but this is not always the case. There is so much that can impact how and with whom we fit in as teens. Another way to promote a false sense of acceptance is to follow the crowd. If friends decide they want to drink, then the thought is to drink. If friends decide they want to do drugs, then the thought is to do drugs. If friends decide that the best way to fit in is to regularly party, then the thought is to regularly party. Again, the danger in this is not just the obvious consequence of the choice, but also the false notion of acceptance. To be excluded by making a separate choice from the group is a big risk. To feel wronged by making a right decision is a heavy burden to carry when acceptance feels so much safer.

What is a teen to do? How do you stand your ground and fit in at the same time? Talk about it. Talk about concerns as a family. Talk about your concerns to your friends. Talk about the risks and potential outcomes of choices. Seek strategies to maintain healthy boundaries and fit in, too. Don't be afraid to openly discuss fears and difficult subjects with parents and/or mentors and caregivers. When teens are left to their own devices to figure out how to navigate such big and potentially damaging situations a lot of bad things can happen. Realize that since there is so much out there that teens have access to today that there is a lot you really don't know, even when you think you do. Trust in this area is not something that can be taken lightly. You can't take anything for granted. Drugs and alcohol are issues where you can be in over your head before you know it. No one should tell you otherwise.

Our local school district hosts a drug awareness day during Red Ribbon Week. It is put on by a local chapter of the SAFE Foundation and it is for eighth grade students and their parents. What the majority of students don't know is that specific students are chosen, along with their parent, to act as plants in a drug demonstration. They set "drugs" out on a table, along with pictures and literature for students to read, view, and touch. When going through the line a student, who is secretly tagged as a "plant," is supposed to take some of the drugs (which are also "plants" in that they are not really drugs but placebos that look like the drugs) when moving through the line. What follows is a mock discovery where the student who took the drug is found out by one of the workers and the local police who are helping with the demonstration are called over to intervene. The script follows with a mock trial and then a mock hospital scene where the student overdoses and the parent doesn't know if the student is going to live or die. Due to the serious nature of the topic, the fact that the eighth graders don't know that the student is a "plant" initially, and the dramatization, it takes some time for the shock to wear off and the whole group of students to catch on to the fact that the scene is somewhat scripted. It has a great impact on the reality of what can happen when kids are careless and cavalier about drugs.

Our oldest son was chosen to be the "plant" with his dad. It was very emotional to keep the secret as well as go through the whole process. We heard from a handful of parents and friends that the fact that Sam was initially the one who got caught with drugs really sunk in with the kids who were unaware that he was acting. The demonstration hit home on many levels for parents and kids alike. Where it benefitted our family was in opening a safe discussion about drugs in general. We were able to talk about all the risks and all the consequences without any sense of interrogation. It also paved the way for our other two kids to participate in the scene as actors when they reached the eighth grade. Again, this kept the discussion of drugs open in our household for many years running. If this is not the case in your family, there are many other ways to broach the subject of drugs.

Because Sam attended the private Catholic high school when he began ninth grade, as a result there was a zero-tolerance policy for not following the rules at the school. When he was a freshman, one of the boys at the school was caught with drugs in his backpack, and he was expelled permanently from the school. We told the story at the dinner table to promote discussion about drugs, rules, and consequences. We tell stories all the time at the dinner table about things that happen, involving drugs and alcohol, with people the kids know around town. This is great for two reasons. It opens up a dialogue that is uncensored and teaches kids that they can talk about anything at any time with you. It also helps them to realize that you know what is going on in town when they may think that you are clueless. It can establish a level of respect and information exchange when your kids realize that you can keep a confidence in regard to touchy subject matters. They will be more apt to share information about people and parties and situations with you when they know that you will not use the information against them or others. I let my kids know, early on, that anything they share with me will always stay with me unless I feel that it is detrimental to the life of another person. If I find that I do need to share a fact then I promise my kids that I will go to them first so they will be kept in the loop if it is critical to divulge information.

When it comes to drinking and drugs, the only way to success-fully navigate is by modeling. I have three non-negotiables for my kids. The first is no drinking and driving under any circumstance at any time. This means I have to give them every option to never make the choice to drink and drive and/or to not get in a car with anyone who has been drinking and driving. I tell them they are allowed to call me as the first option and I will come get them no matter the time or place, no questions or consequences. I also give them a list of names and phone numbers of other people they can call if they do not want to call me. I also set up Uber on each of their phones. The second non-negotiable is no drugs ever. Communication and education reinforce this rule. The other mantra surrounding no drugs is that making the choice to try drugs even just one time could mean that you make the choice to die. I tell them that if they try drugs there is always the potential that it can kill them—either suddenly or by addiction of many forms. The last non-negotiable is that they are not allowed to choose to live with someone they are dating before marriage. This last rule is due to personal experience, religious beliefs, and statistical data. We discuss it in more depth as a family, but my main points as a non-negotiable stand.

My defense in laying down the three non-negotiables is that I will build trust and respect with them as an open and easy parent with minimal restrictions that are only in their best interest. In addition, I build trust and respect by modeling my rules. I never drink and drive just like I ask of my kids. I share stories with them all the time about going out on foot (which is easy to do in our town), or bike. I tell them of times when I have gone out with a car, not expecting to drink, and then calling a friend and leaving my car when I do. I have had my kids drive for me if I drink and on a couple of occasions I have called my kids to come and get me. I also plan ahead by using Uber to get me to and from an outing that is not in town when I know that I am going to be drinking. I believe the only way to get a teen to do what you want them to do is to model the behavior you require of them as well. I think the best way to reinforce modeling is through communication. Call attention to good behaviors in yourself and in your kids. This reinforces positive results and promotes camaraderie.

My kids point out to me when they feel my behavior is inappropriate to them. They have been out with me and some of my good friends when I may drink more than normal. One friend in particular, who we all visit together, is someone that I drink with, tell stories to, and laugh and act silly with. It bothers my daughter sometimes and she has brought it up in the past. I respect her opinion, but I also put it in context. I model all the behaviors I require of my kids when I am with my friend. I do drink more than I normally do when I am with certain friends. If I am following my rules then I think it is important to hear what my kids say about the matter yet also explain my perspective. I am old enough to drink when I choose and sometimes I let my hair down more than average. This means I escape reality a little, am not always "perfect," and indulge in a fairly innocent habit for me under the specific parameters of safe behavior. They need to know that I can follow the rules too, but that I am also allowed to make choices for myself that blur their parental "image" of me. As long as it is a clear, honorable discussion that teaches them that I am as much an imperfect person as any of us, then it can teach a great life lesson. Teach them to be aware, to have opinions, to see whole sides of a situation and find balance in what is true and healthy. This is the key to modeling well with MAPS.

You can do this as a successful parent of teenagers as well. It is never too late to model good behavior. Kids watch everything. They have opinions about everything. Talk. Communicate. Share stories. Live. I recommend not covering up anything in the name of making it look like something that it is not. Modeling shows that we are all willing to tow the line. It shows that our money is where our mouth is, so to speak. The idea that you can ask kids to do as you say and not as you do is not going to work. They will watch what you do and justify many choices by your actions. If you need to change a behavior for your kids, then change it. Talk to them about why you did. It's okay to make a mistake and tell your kids that you made a mistake and then show them how you are going to turn the mistake around moving forward. This is the way to model another great life lesson for teens. They need to see that they can make mistakes and learn from them. They need to know that their expectations of themselves should come from within, not be a line of yours that they are trying to reach. Show them how you set your bar for you and then let them set a bar for themselves that comes from a desire to grow by what they see through you. Once your kids reach the teen years, they can teach us a lot about how to be whole and fully present with them, for them, and in the world at large. Modeling behaviors represents honest effort. Show them that honest effort will always make a difference. It's a sure way to navigate the best of yourself in every moment.

ROAD MAPS

Set standards and model behavior. Always be willing to tackle difficult subjects even when your kids feel uncomfortable about the topic. Express what you know and do not be afraid to ask for clarification and information from them on what you don't know. I find that teens like to be a resource to parents. As you open yourself to what they know, open yourself also to constructive feedback from them regarding your own behaviors. Let your teens know that they can have valid opinions but also focus on context. I am a proponent of modeling but there are reasons why standards of modeling may be slightly justifiable for an adult versus a teen. I will say that justification is not generally true, but in specific cases it can be. The goal of open communication with teens will foster understanding and should go both ways. We are all imperfect so model to the absolute best of your ability and never be afraid to admit and learn from mistakes.

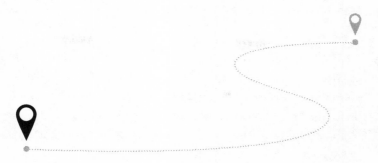

Work and Extracurricular Activities

This is a full topic of conversation with many angles. I must admit up front that my viewpoints on this topic come from a place of sufficiency. I know that is a relative term, but my point is that there was never a time that myself or my kids, when growing up, were required to work for pay in order to meet our basic needs. Though the information is direct, valuable, viable, and true, it is within a very limited vantage point. The concepts apply as far as the integrity of MAPS is concerned, but I in no way assume that the advice aligns with circumstances outside of stereotypical "middle class" suburbia. That being said, the information follows many of my same lines of connecting with your kids to form best decisions and solutions.

When I speak of work and extracurricular activities I approach the topics for parents as well as kids. How we spend our time as a parent—encompassing work, volunteering, child rearing, social-izing, groups, travel, activities, and the like—directly impacts our children. Our ways will carry over into their habits and perceptions of how to spend their own time. It will also affect our image of who we are to our kids and our direct relationship to and with them. Be careful about what you choose to model in this subject area, and most especially, why. Open dialogues about choices are key. Also, be fully present and engage your kids in all of these topic categories. It's tough to teach and balance healthy habits for all and challenging to be aware of our own patterns at times. If your child brings home a drawing of you from school that is a picture of you waving out the window from your car, take a step back and examine whether it's a functional snapshot or a negligent one. This scenario happened to me with my youngest.

For teens, this is the area to speak up. Let teens talk about how they like to spend time and why. Find opportunities to learn new things that spark interest. Help teens practice being bored. Embrace quiet times. Move, work, volunteer, act, serve, and design schedules. Teens should have things to do that are easy, gratifying, challenging, new, contributing, relaxing, necessary, and everything in between. Many of the activities from school, work, and all extracurricular activities aid in building lifelong skills. These categories and skills shape personality surrounding teamwork, motivation, networking, introspection, and individuality. This is also a topic of caution with habits surrounding social media when it comes to extracurricular activities. Don't use social media as a means to make something into something that it is not. Find passions and outlets that are more connective, creative, and stimulating rather than isolating. A measure of how much time spent on social media will give a clear picture of how much time is solitary and/or fabricated. Social media is not interactive in a connective, real way. It's a great place to maximize communication and bridge distance but remember the vehicle is a device that filters away social action and environment. As a rule of thumb, do not write or post anything on social media that you are not willing to say or do directly to someone's face. Also, be careful about the implications of posts. There are many undetected ways to be viewed. Help teens find interest and activities apart from social media and participate regardless of public display. Social media is a whole other side to extracurricular that can be used wisely. Cultivate teen interests in the world itself and grow into the best version of uniqueness and genuine acceptance.

My kids did not have to get jobs as a general rule in our house. They did however, like the idea of earning money. Sam fell into a job both through sports and through volunteering. When he was playing soccer, and then his brother and sister followed, he was asked to become a referee for the micro leagues. It was a great way to earn money and be outside at the same time. It was the perfect schedule for him because the games were on the weekends and fit in around his own sports schedule and never conflicted with school. As he moved from soccer to baseball, he then became a junior umpire and worked games for the younger ages. Both jobs involved training and embodied a code of conduct, so from my perspective they added to my goals in raising healthy teenagers as a parent. It then followed that both his brother and sister had the opportunity to do the same for soccer refereeing.

All of my kids also volunteered during the summer to work a vacation Bible camp that I resurrected and ran at our church. Because of their visible roles within the community, what followed were requests for babysitting, driving friend's kids around, and taking care of pets, all of which generated income for each of them. My daughter also added tutoring to her repertoire and each of them earned money to save and spend as they pleased. It was a nice balance of income and flexibility that helped foster independence and still fit in to their own schedules as desired. Eventually Sam's love of sports and experience working various games landed him a job at our local golf course. Each of the kids would use the money they earned to make personal purchases, buy treats and lunches out, and do fun things.

In addition, we would supplement their income with allowance. I read somewhere that a good strategy to use with kids and allowance is to match their age, dollar per year of age, and offer that amount once a week. The recommendation was to split the allowance into the categories of spend, save, and give. So, for a nine-year-old, give $9 in allowance per week, with $3 going to spending, $3 to saving, and $3 to giving. The other caveat to what we read is to keep allowance as a privilege, not as anything attached to chores. The idea of chores is that they are required to contribute to helping the family as a whole. You take out the trash, empty the dishwasher, clean your room, help in the yard, etc., because you are asked at a certain age to support the family as a whole, not because you are getting money to do so. It teaches the difference between responsibility and privilege. We don't always get paid to follow through with our responsibilities . . . sometimes we just have to contribute for the greater good. So, for a nine-year-old, $12 of spending money per month can be a lot or a little. We would often supplement activities and desires for our kids as necessary. The best part about the whole concept was the open dialogue and teaching moments. We set up checking accounts for each child (they came with us) when we instituted allowance. They would watch their savings grow and then they could use it to make a bigger purchase if we felt it was appropriate. Over time our kids would eventually end up using it for travel with friends. Then twice a year we would take what they saved for giving and we would offer it to church and/or the schools foundation and always to a local family fundraising event for a friend born with Type 1 diabetes. All in all, the jobs and the allowance were a great model for our kids and worked well for each one.

I mentioned travel as an area where our kids would spend the bulk of their saved money. Travel is big in our family. We would plan annual trips to Disneyland, skiing, and camping when our kids were growing up. They would travel with friend's families occasionally.

Shaun had a couple of amazing opportunities to travel with my parents overseas due to the fact that he was not yet in high school, so missing classes was not a huge detriment. There was a time when I would take "girls trips" once a year, for my own personal fun and breaks. All of these extracurricular activities can be teaching moments in a positive way. I believe it is important for kids to see that parents need appropriate outlets for independent time away from family. Taking care of self is a necessary message to instill in kids in a healthy way. Occasional travel, nights out, and exercise are all great ways to model independent needs within the family.

When the kids were little I would often choose to go out with friends if I knew I would be home for bedtime routine. Or I would go after bedtime. I always chose to exercise in the early morning hours so it would not take away my time from home and on some mornings this meant that their dad would do breakfast and lunch duty and then I would be home to see them off. For the trip away with my girlfriends, I was able to show my kids that I could have fun without them but it in no way impacted my love or desire for them. I would return home missing them greatly and they could see that I would come back after leaving and that all was still well. This concept is true of work as well. The choices we make in spending our time are ultimately big picture choices. How do we support our minds, our family, our body, and our life as a whole? Show kids that time away from family is sometimes necessary. Go back to the cost/ benefit. Adapt to requirements for living and show that adjustments can be made, obligations prioritized, and commitments balanced. Each person is an individual and also part of a group. The individuals need to be well for the group to thrive.

I did not always offer the best picture of how to appropriately balance work and extracurricular activities. I feel like I do now. Initially as a stay-at-home-mom, volunteer, marathon/half marathon runner, worker outside the home, socializer, traveler, and many other fly-by-the-seat-of-your-pants responsibilities, my habits and choices became my routine for everyday living. I did a lot of justifying. I would justify time away. I would justify that things had to get done around the house before I could focus attention elsewhere. "Just give me a sec" was my mantra and my kids quickly learned that a "sec" meant a minimum of fifteen minutes and would often end in the forgotten fact that they needed my help and attention. I would sometimes realize the next day that I forgot to get back to them. At that point, my apologies were hollow.

What did work for us were camping trips, vacations with other families, and annual traditions. Routines provided structure and distraction. They created an energy that took on a life of its own. Even my schedule that I used on my first two kids had to morph with the third child. When it came time for his naps, I would often have to be in the car picking up another sibling. Or it would be library time with my daughter. Shaun was the only one of my kids who I had to lay down with to eventually get him to take naps. He still likes when things are done for him and he is the most "spoiled" of his siblings in this way. Yet, he is also the child who taught me the most about slowing down. About focus. About presence. Since he demanded all of me, I had to teach myself to give him all of me. I took a good, hard look at what was so important to me that I could not give him my full attention. I realized gradually, as my other kids got older and more independent, that time stands still for no one and that I was going to miss out on the years with them all if I continued my pace and misguided priorities. I held a small mirror up to myself that turned into a big mirror during my divorce.

Going through the divorce was not an easy process. In order to mitigate as much discord as possible for the kids, their father and I were the ones who initially switched in and out of our home and shared a studio so the kids could stay put in their familiar place. We did this for over a year. When I was forced to live in the silence of a studio, alone, I quickly learned that my social "yeses" were knee-jerk responses to relationship survival mode. When I didn't have to insulate my marriage, I could actually sit back and determine if my choices were a good use of time. Many of them were not. I pulled way back socially and took a look at all of my activities, friendships, and obligations through a more authentic lens. What I am now left with is mostly healthy, balanced tasks and people.

Adaptation is the key component of MAPS for work and extra-curricular activities. I mention in another chapter about scheduling at least one family meal together. If dinner doesn't work, then make it breakfast. This may be the only way to adapt to the possibility of a family meal for work schedules and/or extracurricular conflicts. Also, with multiple siblings, schedules need to constantly adapt. What is perfect for the first child is not always doable with successive siblings. Adapt. Keep the same concept but modify the rigidity. Make two naps into one longer one, shift mealtime, slacken the requirements of when and how chores need to be done. Take breaks.

I remember one year we chose not to have my daughter play on her high school soccer team. She was a sophomore, finished her fall club season, and wasn't ready to jump into another season with her school. When we sat down to evaluate the necessity we realized that this was the perfect time for her to step back a little. There would be no negative impact from a prospective college level, she played on the varsity team as a freshman, they had a strong team that was senior heavy during her sophomore year so she could simply sit out high school soccer and pick up as a strong varsity player her junior year. Adapt. I transitioned some volunteer obligations at the church and let go of some of my PTA responsibilities and only focused on classroom time as my older kids moved out of elementary school. Adapt.

It is important to constantly look at why we do the things we do with our time and the cost/benefit. If something no longer retains priority status, drop it or change it. Teach your kids how to adapt homework priorities as well. Simple acts of balancing homework requirements, reaching out to teachers with sensible, pertinent requests, can teach kids how to advocate for themselves and learn balance through adaptation as well. Institute family nights. Be bored. Rest. There were times when I would read novels out loud to my kids to slow myself down and be present to them. Find ways that work best for your family and honor them for yourself and for your kids.

Though the focus for success with MAPS and work/extracurricular is adaptation, as parents the best way to teach adaptation is to model behavior. I share stories above of both my kids and myself, because the key to teaching them how to live well is showing them how to live well. This is also an area where you have to let your kids teach you. I tell my children often that they reach a point in their lives where they have ways to show me that what I am doing is good or bad, right or wrong. In the beginning I mentioned the picture from my son . . . pretty insightful for a kindergartener. In their young adult years, the request for my full attention taught me indirectly. To this day, comments from my kids about why I am in such a hurry when I am in the car or why I have to make judgmental comments about people I do not know when their actions have no effect on me teach me ways to evaluate the best use of my time and energy. Let your kids be a gauge, but then you be an example. Show them that you can adapt, should adapt, and will adapt to meet needs and become a more balanced, whole, intentional person overall. Adaptation will serve everyone well.

ROAD MAPS

Adaptation and a two-way mirror are key when it comes to extra-curricular activities and work. Our kids will most likely always want more of our time than we can sometimes give, but if it is a consistent request, evaluate priorities. Beware of falling into patterns of always doing the same thing. Every time you sign up for or renew an activity ask if it makes sense for the time at hand. It may be something to drop or change or simply break from for a while. Instill work ethic where possible. This starts in the home, can equate to volunteering, and lead to work for pay. When teens earn their own money it can be motivating and empowering. All in all, the focus is on balance and intention. Adapt, model, and slow down when necessary.

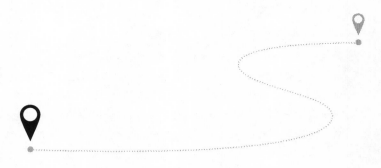

Divorce

Divorce is a topic that came up shortly after I began writing submissions for my book. There was a conversation about whether or not the entire book should offer parenting advice to families affected by divorce. I immediately responded that so much parenting took place for fifteen years before the divorce caused a break in our family unit that it was not the divorce that was the focus, just a component. Though divorce is never ultimately a choice we want to make, it is possible to navigate with a level of health and success. The discussion did make me realize that it is possible to raise healthy kids in the midst of and through divorce. The key is with MAPS and a little finesse.

To me personally, divorce felt like a dirty word. I even choose to not call my former spouse my ex-husband. When I refer to him, almost always, I will refer to him as the father of my children. Part of the reason why is because I can't stand the thought of fitting into the aspect of divorce that involves a cliché term, such as "my ex." I am extremely sensitive to stereotypes in various ways. The idea of divorce has never been looked on favorably in my upbringing, mainly due to religious beliefs in my immediate family. In my extended family, every single couple in my grandparents' and parents' generation kept an intact, legal, and proximal union through marriage. I called off an engagement, six weeks prior to the wedding, because I knew in my heart that I would not be able to stay married to the person forever. The fact that I initiated, acted, and finalized my own divorce was never in the realm of thinking for me until I was forced to face the reality of circumstances regarding my engagement, wedding, and marriage of seventeen years. My marriage was annulled on a sacramental level, so as far as I am concerned I have no ex-husband. I really do only have three great kids and their father who helped me create and raise them. If anyone chooses to say that annulment invalidates children, the opposite is actually true, it puts the emphasis on the fact that there is a mother and father who had children together, regardless of the presence of a sacramental, legal, marital union.

As parents who have experienced divorce, we all have our unique stories and set of circumstances. Divorce is perceived by many to be mostly negative because it sheds light primarily on the brokenness of a couple's marriage. It can also discount a parent's confidence through fights, accusations, lies, gossip, access to children, finances, comforts, stability, connection, stress, vulnerability, uncertainty, judgment, and the like. Sometimes divorce is mutual, sometimes one-sided, sometimes reactive, impulsive, a cop-out, or sometimes it is necessary. No matter what the reason, divorce is generally messy and carries a lot of social stigma. As a parent the social perceptions can create a lot of loose cannons, and I would caution against caring about anything other than how to maintain the best concept as possible of "family" and stability for your kids.

Divorce is an adult choice, one that falls solely to the parents. It may not always be a mutual choice between two parents, but it is a mutual responsibility by nature of kids. We are called as parents to be mature through divorce for our kids and to take on the bulk of the burden by the fact that we are not just individual adults but caregivers. Parents are the ones who need to make the sacrifices in order to minimize the experience of a broken family for our children. It is very easy to say and much more difficult to practice yet critical to raising healthy, balanced kids.

From a children's perspective the act of divorce can be debilitating. Even situations where safety may be the guiding factor there is generally always a rhythm of life present that the kids consciously or subconsciously depend on for definition (identity) and practice (routine). Our family is a foundation whether it is rocky or stable, authentic or imagined, and any imbalance in the foundation challenges our perceptions of everything. The idea that a parents' marriage cannot withstand all a child knows of family can be crushing. Divorce changes a known, perceived state of reality in which a family unit functions, even if it is in a dysfunctional way, and brings up anxiety and questions as to the cause. Divorce creates an extreme break in status quo, fuels anxiety, and questions perceptions that are often the basis of self that children begin to stand for and function with wholeheartedly.

Kids often feel that they are responsible for the break, begin to see themselves differently, question safety through the vulnerability of upset, imagine nothing is stable or real, and that people will see them negatively in ways they don't want to imagine. It is a tainted feeling, much like my own perception of divorce being dirty; a non-solution. The child's world is shattered beyond control and they are forced to begin again, often without warning. The divorce may feel like a necessary solution to the parents yet it may be anything but for the kids. Even if the divorce makes sense there is a huge rift and a big shift in family dynamics. An often-sacred unit is now in shambles. One of the biggest fears surrounding all three of my children at the beginning of the divorce was how much change would seep into their world that they only wished to stay the same.

I have a story for each one of my kids that represents a different aspect of our divorce. The first is a story of my oldest, just weeks after

I initiated the family talk to make the announcement. We purposely waited until the school year was over. We did not want to impact the kids and their focus, efforts, and energy as students. We figured the start of summer would give all of us a chance to process the enormous shift in family life before any energy needed to be expended back to school life. We all sat down together and let the kids know we needed to have a family talk. The responsibility to initiate and deliver the news was on me as I was the only one in our family who was making the choice for divorce.

I began by stating to the kids that I had something to tell them that I never expected I would have to say at this point in my life. I let them know that it was not a decision I ever wanted to make or was making lightly, but that I did believe it was the best decision for everyone moving forward. I then told them that I was asking for a divorce and that I was so sorry it had come to be that this was going to be a new reality for all of us. There were immediate tears and very little questions. I think I remember continuing to speak, but I have no idea what I was saying. At one point, their dad went off with them and I later learned that he told them a version of not wanting the divorce, not believing in divorce, and going through with everything because of my choice only. All of those statements were true, but in retrospect, it was non-disclosed to me at the time and inaccurately shaped my own motivations, perceived by the kids, which I share only because as I continuously stood in my convictions throughout the entire situation, there has been much impact on what prevailed of which I was unaware for some time. I know too that it permeates throughout my community of life, due to the fact that two people deal with situations the way they best see fit. In the case of divorce, I implore you to always put your kids first, and leave personal interpretations and judgments personal. A one-sided story is never a true story. It is simply one side of a true story.

I was driving around one day with Sam and decided to check in with how he was doing after the discussion about the divorce. I asked him if he had any questions. I wanted to know where his mind was with everything because he is always honest with me and a good gauge of whether or not the heart of what I try to say or do gets across in the manner I wish. I also wanted him to know that I was there for him, as I have always promised my kids, in any way, shape, or form. They know they can come to me for any reason, even when it has to do with negative feedback or constructive criticism. It is something I try to reinforce as an open door, but I also realize there are times when I need to solicit feedback because it is not always easy to approach a parent about an uncomfortable topic. He shared his thoughts without reservation, being honest about the shock and also about his under-standing. He is very insightful by nature. His comment to me about how I presented my announcement about the divorce surprised me. He said that when I began by stating that I had something to share with them that I never expected to at this point in my life, he thought that I was going to tell them all that I was pregnant.

My main point in sharing this story is that it reinforces my belief that kids want, above all else, a grounded, stable family life. I feel they wish for this security and foster it, even under less than ideal, and in certain instances, unsafe environments. Children endure and develop in response to support their sense of family, so the last thing that was on the minds of any of my kids when I delivered the news of a break up was the subject of divorce. My oldest son thought that I was pregnant, even though they were surrounded by our recent discord, fighting, and subtle separation, and the fact that we had never, ever breathed a word about wanting more kids. Our youngest was already ten, but it made more sense that more kids would enter the picture as an option than the consideration of divorce.

A short story about how important it is to keep the kids out of the middle of parental battles during divorce is to foster a show of "respect" for one another by keeping kids out of the middle of messy details. Put them first by keeping their lives as straightforward as possible. To honor this, we took our divorce in phases. We began by keeping our kids in their home for the first year of the separation. We did this by renting a studio that we both shared, and I would stay there for one week and then switch home for a week, alternating with their dad. This was a good idea for two reasons. The first is that is kept the kids settled in their routines, minimally disrupted their schedules and kept them in a familiar, comfortable place while dealing with immense change otherwise. The second is that it gave me and their dad insight into how stressful and draining switching homes can be on a regular basis. It is a very unsettling feeling that is disjointing in a lot of ways. When it came time for our kids to switch on and off each week, we could empathize and help mitigate what they were taking on.

On top of phasing into different living environments, we required they each go to a counselor at least twice so they knew they always had that as an option. We vowed to leave them out of any and all discussions about the details of the divorce and our feelings about one another unless they asked (and to tread lightly when approached). It was very important that we not make negative comments about the other parent because kids have no recourse when that happens, it only makes them feel insecure and vulnerable—like they are being forced to agree or disagree and somehow pick a side. Shaun received a phone call from his dad one night. The three kids and I were all sitting on the couch together so it was easy to hear his side of the conversation. He sounded irritated and was being short with his dad. He also kept repeating, "I know," in response to whatever was being said. I couldn't help but hear the dealings from Shaun's side of the call and my immediate reaction, and past role in such circumstances, was to swoop in and make everything better. When Shaun hung up the phone I asked what I could do to help him and he looked right at me and said, "Mom, this is none of your business, it's between me and Dad."

My first instinct was to be hurt and try to defend myself, but as I sat there for a second I realized instantly that he was right. It had nothing to do with me at all. In fact, part of the reasoning behind why I chose divorce while all of my kids were still living at home was because I felt it was important for them to be able to assimilate to a new way of "family" life while they were still in the only phase of life they knew. For my own circumstances, I did not see the value in waiting for them all to leave for college. I wanted to have situations come up that we all got used to while everyone of us was still in close proximity. The bold nature of Shaun's statement supported my reasoning and also forced me to live my own version of it by respecting boundaries. My kids needed to learn how to foster relationship with each of their parents as separate entities. It was no longer my role to "fix" a potential pitfall. What I had tried to cover up in the past was now in the hands of the kids and their individual interactions with each of us as parents, and Shaun's declaration genuinely acknowledged the truth of it all.

I mentioned that counseling was something that we made each of the kids do, at least two times, shortly after I announced the divorce. We wanted the kids to know that they had the option of talking to a trained, objective psychologist to help them through the process of divorce. We took the initiative as parents to find the doctors, consult with them, and then let the kids go one-on-one to two mandatory visits. All three kids decided they did not want to continue counseling immediately after the two visits. About a month later, Shaun decided that he wanted to go again, so we took him to about three more visits at his request. He has not asked to go back up to this point. Sarah decided about a year later that she wanted to find her own female counselor. She went to a woman, who was younger, for a couple of months, and she felt like it wasn't the right connection or perspective so she stopped.

A few months later we found, through several recommendations, a woman who was younger, happily married with kids, who Sarah now really admires and respects. She saw her for a year, as a senior in high school, on a weekly basis and continues to check in on visits home, as she schedules herself. Having a place to objectively share her thoughts and feelings has been very positive for Sarah. It has helped to build her confidence, provide a forum for safe disclosure, and it gives her permission to stand for her own opinion under circumstances where she may otherwise feel like she has to comply. I highly recommend exposing your kids to the option of counseling. It is necessary to stay active in a peripheral part of the process and also to ensure that the therapist is providing an environment that is safe, respectful, and in line with the core values you wish for your kids to aspire.

In some ways the therapist can compliment the concept of MAPS. I believe this is the case with Sarah and her counselor. We have had a handful of productive conversations that stemmed from Sarah's sessions. One that stands out is unique in that Sarah was actually able to teach me a lesson where I took a step back, absorbed the viewpoint, and softened my mindset in an area where I have been struggling as well. My extended family of origin lives locally. My parents are both in town as well as my sister, her husband, and three girls. We are a stereotypical Italian family. My parents, who are retired, like to stay busy by helping out with their grandkids. My dad will be the first to admit, as he did those first few years with grandkids, that had he known how much fun grandkids could be he would've had them first. The comment is both funny and true; raising kids brings so much more risk, effort, and energy along with it than spending time with grandkids on any level. They have always been and continue to be there for their grandkids in any way possible. We are blessed by the support and the bond, yet at times it can act as interference and become added stress—especially when it compromises my direction and relationship with the kids.

I was sharing a frustration with Sarah about an area where my parents overstepped their role and I was letting out emotion and history surrounding my feelings. Sarah pointed out to me that she had been talking to her counselor about the role of family in her own life. She shared that just because you have an idea of what you want your family to be like doesn't change the fact that you still have two parents. When we evolve through our own families we may have to tweak the definition due to various factors. She shared that it doesn't change who your parents are, it just changes who they are to you in the current space and time. How wise and mature she sounded to me as she delivered a message I needed to hear as much as she did, but for so many different reasons.

Divorce breaks families, but it doesn't change who we have as parents. Many things have the capacity to break families but it is possible to evolve through issues to a higher level. MAPS forces us to grow constantly by the very nature of what it requires. To model, adapt, participate and slow down means we are forced to evaluate who, what, where, why, and how against a myriad of situations. We have choices to make, each new day, which involve action, consequence, and outcome. Modeling behavior challenges our insecurities, weaknesses, and comforts. Adaptation demands perspective that is not always our own. All of my kids teach me daily, broaden my patterns of thinking, and help me become a better version of myself through participation. On top of all of this insight and evolution is the looking glass of slowing down. Without pause, we continue headlong and headstrong on a road that may lead us far from where we want to be unless we analyze the route.

Divorce marks a detour in the course of our normal route. My best advice in this situation is to analyze the root to find a new route that better meets the needs of all involved. Since there are so many circumstances that perpetuate divorce, getting at the root of the matter is key. I recommend healthy counseling options for everyone.

I believe in putting the well-being and stability of your children's environments before your own whenever possible. Divorce is one area that seeing things from the side of your kids can help mitigate unnecessary discord. It requires a lot of self-sacrifice up front but in the long run may make for better relationships than ever imaginable. Communicate, love, support, and heal by facing fear, asking for help, and standing convicted. It's a very windy road but it can lead to new heights. It's not a course I would ever intend to take but it could wind up being a hidden gem that is a little off the beaten path.

ROAD MAPS

Be open rather than transparent. It is critical to communicate and be accessible. It is not necessary to divulge personal details. Make the kids first priority and take on self-sacrifice for the greater good. Just as kids have no choice about being brought into the world, they have no choice in divorce so mitigate discord. Offer a channel of objective communication through counseling. Work together as much as possible to keep "family." It may be necessary to put on a poker face when out and about at venues where everyone will be together after divorce but that is the role of a parent. If you are not able to interact amiably then just stay separate, but still participate in presence. Work in phases if you can, and be cognizant of what is going on in the lives of your teens. At the same time, recognize that your child will need a time to define a new normal, and actively participate in making this happen. Divorce is never easy but it can be managed well.

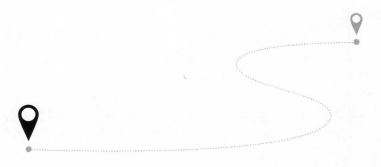

College

The idea of whether or not to attend college and where to go is a very filled topic with lots of angles to consider. One thing I know for certain is that it is best to let the attendee take the lead down this path. The decision works when motivated by personal desire and interest. Parents may have very set ideas about expectations in the area of college and we all know my thoughts on expectations—they are personal and subjective, and they impose misplaced and often misinterpreted judgment on another. It is one thing to have a family legacy to a specific college that may benefit subsequent generations and carry on positive tradition, yet such a notion applies to an extremely small percentage of cases that could refute my advice on the matter. The goal in raising teens is to allow them to develop personal motivation and self-sufficiency as they grow out into the world. College can be a great first stepping-stone toward individual, "real world" success, so the choice and interest should rest primarily within the teen.

Also, this is an area where every child will have a different path and unique sense of process and discovery. Parents are encouraged to plant seeds, foster interests, and verbalize suggestions but the follow through should come from the teens themselves. I will also note that this is another area where finances can dictate and override ultimate choices and I do not pretend to ignore the pressures and constraints of a financial bottom line. However, had I been made aware of all of my options in the area of finances for school, I may have chosen a much different path than the one I felt was necessary for me to pick. Give your child every option available to achieve their dreams. When that is just not possible in terms of dollars, then the choice may be one that is dictated due to the factor of money. That is okay, too. Sometimes we don't realize that what seems like a second choice is actually the best one of all until we experience it firsthand. I repeat my two main points when I say let the child take the lead and communicate and support every option available to help them reach their dreams. Also, my disclaimer is worth repetition in that I speak from personal experience and do not pretend to take in the myriad situations that involve impossible financial barriers that one is not able to escape.

College is a charged topic. It is an involved process. It is stressful, overwhelming, tedious, exciting, and rewarding. It is the first world, in most cases, beyond home for the teen. It is the true start to them actually becoming their own "family" so to speak. It opens up a whole new world for the family dynamic in general and can have as much of an impact on the teen going off as to the members of the family left behind. It is a topic area that requires great sensitivity, patience, and awareness. Go with the flow. Remember, too, that there will not only be a change once the child ventures on (to college or otherwise), but also when they return home for periods of time (whether for vacation, summers, or holidays and gatherings) as they are now independent, or at least dependently independent. It is important to foster individual growth at every turn and continue to offer love and support overall.

There are many layers to the decision about whether or not to attend college or choose a different route. Often it is automatically assumed that a child will attend college but do not let that be a detriment to self-discovery or inhibit personal dreams. College is not the ideal situation for everyone. It can be the best choice for some, a means to an end for others, or an unnecessary option for an alternate post-secondary school path. Best-case scenario involves a formulation of internal motivations and desires throughout the teen years that point to a marker toward future success. Some teens know exactly what they want to be at a very early age. They know if and where they would like to go for college. They have a specific interest in a vocation, sport, subject, and/or career that can make the process clear, methodical, and straightforward. Other teens have multiple interests and talents that conflict, easily work together, or have nothing to do with baccalaureate schooling whatsoever. Then there are teens who have no idea what they want to do, where they want to go, or how to make it all work. In each case, it is okay. No teen should really be expected to know what they want to do or where they want to go when they are seventeen, and if they happen to know it is all right if it changes once they embark into the world at large.

What is important is to communicate and experience appropriate thoughts and interests whenever possible. Middle school and high school can be a great backdrop for exploration. Volunteer, work different jobs, take lessons, play sports, travel, read, watch, and learn in all the ways that stimulate curiosity. Trial and error are great ways to navigate experiences and forge unique goals just right for you. Ask questions and talk to family, friends, and mentors. All of it will teach verbal communication skills, confidence, networking, interviewing, and the like throughout the years. Figure out how to work best and what you enjoy most along the way. All of these things will contribute to a step in future direction.

I am coming at this topic with a lot of personal history. I knew that I was going to attend college and I knew that I wanted to when I was a teen. I thought that I wanted to be an attorney so I applied to colleges as a pre-law major. My first choice was a to go to a local, prestigious, private university to which I was accepted. I also applied to a handful of other colleges and after other options added to the list, my parents suggested a trip to tour some of the campuses in person. Even though I got accepted to my top choice, and the university was the closest of all my options, we did not tour that campus. We went to three other campuses in the northern part of California. Of all the three, I liked the one that was farthest from home, and the largest, because of the buildings and grounds of the campus and surrounding town. It was an off-the-radar state school at the time, and I convinced myself that it was perfect because it was the exact opposite of where I grew up and I was kind of "over" many of the stereotypical makings of small town, Southern California suburbia.

I was not asked what my first choice of college was that would best suit me and my interests. I was not told how much money was set aside for me to attend college. I was not informed of nor did I know that I could apply for college aid loans on my own, and for myself. I was shy, insecure, sheltered, and expected to comply. So, that is what I did—what we all did as a family in a subconscious, habitual, dysfunctional, copasetic way. My ideal college-bound goals were not openly exchanged or acknowledged. In keeping with my family role and my own way, I convinced myself that the college I attended was the ultimate choice for me. It was not. Not only did I immediately find out that I was ill-prepared to navigate myself and life outside my own home, but the campus was too large, I had no transportation of my own, I was two hours away from the closest airport, and over nine hours away from home by car.

In the middle of my college years, my parents moved to the East Coast. My sister joined me at the same college for her first two years until I graduated, but by then I was on an unhealthy spiral both emotionally and academically. I changed my major to psychology, continued to get lost socially (as I was in high school), developed severe, clinical depression that went unrecognized for over twelve years, and missed graduation requirements by two credits, of which I did not find out about from my advisor until the middle of summer after walking graduation. I went back to the same campus for a grad school program, to which my college mentor for the Pupil Personnel Services Credential (my new dream job path) had told me I was accepted, only to find out that the information was inaccurate based on my cumulative test score on the GRE (for which he had looked only at one subject score and could not change the minds of the acceptance committee for the current semester), then lasted through one year of non-specific graduate classes and left for good, with the intention of finishing the program after a few years of work and never finding the right timing to do such a thing.

Avoid this scenario at all costs. Communicate with your children. Encourage dialogue. Listen and guide. Prompt them to develop interests and goals and step them through responsibility. Let them make mistakes and face consequences. Model advocating for them and then hand it over and watch them advocate for themselves during the time of life at home. I am not one to look back on life with regret and I do not agree with the notion that everything happens for a reason. I believe that good can come out of almost any situation at some point in time if we work toward that end. With that being said, I do think, if given the choice, I would not hesitate to change my college years. I have been given a lot of blessings through my kids and college, with their choices of schools, their successes within the colleges they attend, and the scholarships they earned that help tremendously with tuition expenses. So, maybe, that is the good that is coming out of my own college experience. It is honestly the first time I have been able to say so, and for that I am grateful.

Sam has a similar story with his college of choice as he did with the high school that he attended. It initially was not on his radar as a top choice, but it was on his list after discovery. Before he got accepted to the college, and after touring the campus (at the end of a whirlwind, family, college tour trip), it became one of his top two campuses. He applied early action, got accepted, applied for a full tuition scholarship to the university through his high school, and less than a month later was granted the scholarship award. Before final acceptance he found out that he was accepted to a top three, nationally ranked program of study at his other university of choice and by then it was just icing on the cake for him, as he already knew he belonged at the other university from the minute he set foot on the campus during his initial tour. He has since followed a clear and intended path through the business school and will graduate with a double major in management and marketing, with a minor in data analytics, which he wants to use in a sports environment. He has worked for the athletic department since his freshman year, experienced the ultimate in college sports championships, and made lifelong friends. He is proud to represent his university, excels in his classes, and continues to grow into a more responsible, mature, contributing citizen and individual.

He is independent in his college world. He maintains a long-distance relationship with his high school girlfriend, stays in touch with his family regularly, and makes so many of his decisions for himself. He is one of those kids who knew what he wanted to do in college and where he wanted to go to school in general. He has said since the beginning of high school that he wanted to do something with sports and business in college. He also knew that he wanted to go to school somewhere on the East Coast. He applied to eight schools up and down the entire east side of the country. He was self-motivated through the entire process. I took a hands-on and hands-off approach with him. I set up sessions to help with essay writing for the applications. I suggested a university I wanted him to apply to and add to his list. We had conversations about pros and cons of various colleges, locations, and climates. We discussed programs, options, finances, and timelines. The rest of the process was all his follow-through. He made it easy for all of us in many ways. There was some luck and timing mixed into all the details, responsibilities, and requirements. In the end the payoff was that he didn't shy away from any of the responsibility. He has one more year to complete his undergraduate college journey. He is still going strong down his original path. He is away from home this entire summer, working an internship with a professional sports team. I believe it is his first of many summers away as he continues to build his young adult life. I am thankful for and proud of his determination and hard work to continuously achieve his goals and form his future.

My daughter just completed her first year at a top twenty university. She sets her sights high and works to achieve them, all while staying grounded and true to herself. Her story is very different than her older brother's, but no less self-motivated. On some level it was more so, simply because she attended the local public high school versus her brother and his private high school, in which there was a substantial difference in the counseling and academic support. She had dreams of playing soccer in college and that was her goal and process in the beginning phases of applying to colleges. She picked schools from all over the country based on academics and sports programs. Her intention was to play soccer for a D3 university as well as to pursue a degree that would lead her to medical school. Soccer was her driving factor in a choice for which colleges to apply and the other areas rounded out the whole package.

She taught us a lot about the effort involved in reaching out to and connecting with college coaches. There was a lot more to address on top of the application process in general. It was necessary to create and send video footage to coaches, write emails, make phone calls, set up personal visits, and attend ID camps. She needed to be intentional in her selection of camps and travel because of the costs involved. Unfortunately, in the two years prior to graduating high school she was plagued with injuries from her favorite sport. One year, she was not able to play for her high school team due to an injury. By the time she started applying to colleges she was already behind in forging relationships with coaches because of all her injuries. Over the course of two full club soccer seasons, she was injured four times. The last injury resulted in surgery and led to the decision to forgo playing soccer as a college athlete.

She was hit-and-miss with her acceptances to many of the colleges she applied because all of her choices of colleges were very competitive on entrance requirements. She ended up with two top choices, just like her brother, but mixed into that was acceptances to honors programs at some of the colleges on her list. With the honors programs she was offered great financial assistance. Her desire to attend her top choice of schools was now mixed with desirable offers from competing choices, no ability to play soccer at her college anymore, and a higher price tag for tuition to her top schools. The decision was made in the end by looking at every possible angle. We took a trip back to the university she is now attending because her first experience was through the eyes of a soccer ID camp where she lived and breathed everything a collegiate athlete would take part. Next came an extensive financial comparison. There were also visits to colleges she applied and had not yet seen in person before her acceptance. In the end, her decision came down to the wire. She received a letter in the mail, before the decision deadline, informing her that she was the recipient of a full tuition scholarship to her top school. We never dreamed of the possibility that two amazing windfalls would bestow our family. It has been affirming for many reasons. It highlights for me that in looking back on all of my own life I would choose to reach these milestones again and again, so for that I would choose to not change a moment.

As I finish writing this last topic I am beginning to navigate the path to college with my youngest son. It is already significantly different than the other two routes. He has little clarity on where he wants to go and what he would like to study. At sixteen, I tell him all the time that it is not necessary to impose a demand for specific insights at this point in time. He thinks that he wants to play soccer in college. He, like my daughter, loves the sport and plays it well. They have both played soccer as their primary sport of choice since the age of four. He has no specific idea which part of the country suits him best for college, but instead is focusing on various combinations of what he considers to be a whole package with his list of choices. He is interested in sciences but also has a very creative side that is important for him to cultivate. He likes balance and camaraderie so may fit best at a small school with the right mix of sports and academics.

He also thrives on a go-with-the-flow momentum as long as there are set plans, guidelines, and deadlines so a sports focus combined with his area of study may be the most motivating environment for him. He has the extra work, as his sister did, cut out for him with reaching out to college soccer coaches on top of the normal application process. He has been on an academy soccer team for the last three years so he is used to a demanding extracurricular schedule. In addition, he attends games and tournaments that are regularly out of the state. Prior to the start of this past year it was necessary for him to miss a week of school, before finals, to participate in a college soccer showcase in Florida. Upon his return, he had to make up the work he missed during the week he was gone, study for finals, and send emails to college coaches to foster relationships with the coaches he asked to come watch him at the tournament. He was swamped with work and stressed.

At one point, just before his first final, we argued over the fact that I was not helping him write letters to the coaches. He told me that so many of the players were talking about how their parents were writing the emails to the coaches for them and acting as though it was coming from the player themselves. He complained that his dad and I were not doing that for him and it was making him mad because he felt it was unfair. I told him that I understood a lot of what he was communicating to me, and most especially his level of frustration over his stress and the injustice. I told him that some of those kids were going to get into those colleges based on the fact that parents wrote letters to coaches for them and pushed in a specific direction to be noticed and get on a radar. I told him that I would never want that way for him, and that I too think it is unfair. What I want for him is to learn how to manage life through personal responsibility, internal desire, and self-effort. I told him that it was my feeling that he might stand out on his own if he emailed the coaches personally after finals, explained how he was balancing soccer, studies, and his interest in reaching out to the coach in a way that felt like the best way for him to prioritize his efforts. In doing so, perhaps he would differentiate himself from the barrage of emails from other players and his true voice might sound.

The other side of such a hope is that there will be players whose parent's emails sent on their behalf stand out easily and get them into the college. The same parents are on the coach about playtime and exposure and preferential treatment even though the clubs say they don't stand for such a thing. Life works that way all the time, but it is not what I would like to have happen for my own kids. Don't get me wrong, I help and support them, connect them, and do things for them in many ways in order to model behaviors that I want to see develop in intended ways. I won't act on their behalf through misrepresentation. I also stopped speaking on behalf of my son to the coaches and teachers once he reached high school. I speak to my kids and they speak from me in ways they decide are important. I will support them in every way without interceding. I want them to stand for themselves with me so I am reassured that they can do it when they are without me. That is the point of the teen years to me . . . going from prepubescent child to capable, young adult. I will sit next to them as they type, offer wisdom, and help collaborate on best ways to communicate. I will participate as an assistant. Then I will listen to their insights and suggestions on the matter and work with them, not in place of them. I don't want to see them end up somewhere that I want them to be and have them find out when they get there that it was not their desire after all.

The key component of MAPS for navigating the prospect of college is to adapt. Be open to the voice of your teen. Pay attention to their likes, dislikes, weaknesses, and strengths. Hone skills, model behaviors, and participate in interests. Show them you care and that you believe in them in all ways possible. Advocate for them through exposure and then step aside and watch for a while. I think that it is wise for the parent to adapt and let the teen cultivate. Once cultivation takes place in areas of personal interests, then you can model and participate and evaluate as necessary. The concept of slow down can line up with adapt by looking at ways to focus energy in the right places. When your teen gets spread too thin or stressed from keeping too many balls in the air then adapt by prioritizing. Teach them how to discern on their own with strategies that work within the family. We use a list of pros and cons and also rely on prayer and a realistic response time for making decisions. It is okay to teach teens that it can often be appropriate to ask for more time to make a decision in certain situations and with good reason. Sometimes the answer will be no, but it never hurts to ask for best-case scenarios. It is best-case scenarios that we are looking for when talking about this topic. College is not for everyone. Also, every college is not for everyone. As with most topics in this book, talk early and talk often. Be a sounding board and be a support. These are the times where every moment can count for good. Our teens will not be around forever, but we do want them happy, successful and always coming back for more.

ROAD MAPS

Advocate for your kids when it comes to college and refrain from acting on their behalf. Set up options. Communicate clearly about financial support, realities, and possibilities. Discuss desires about college and consider whether or not it is an appropriate option. Be open to various paths. Encourage your kids and help them with resources for support in place of pressure. There is a whole world of sources available when it comes to college, so ask other parents for advice, network, attend fairs, and do research. All efforts will pay off in some way if you remember that self-motivation is key. Adapt by helping to manage priorities, and introduce and create choices even if there is a be-all-end-all focus. You never know where the road may lead.

Death

My mantra throughout this book has been to communicate openly with your kids about all subject matters. No parent enjoys talking about the subject of death. Parents often shield kids from every aspect of death by hiding it from them. Especially in the case of pets by managing the tragedy through a sugar-coated disappearance. We go to great lengths to hide, bury, and somehow dispose of cherished pets, no matter how big or small. It is not as easy to navigate in the case of a loved one but we still manage different ways of minimizing the sad truth of the matter. It is instinctual to protect kids from heartache and sadness, so a tale seems to make it easier on everyone. Sensitivity and anxiety levels of our children can vary greatly so it is not surprising that our gut tells us to avoid as much reality about death as possible. The subject of death is not only something we want to protect kids from but it is a topic that a large number of adults find to be extremely uncomfortable as well. This is true, too, through the context of our own immortality, and how our kids will survive if we die prematurely. So, the topic of death seems something best avoided altogether.

No child normally chooses to openly discuss the topic of death. The teen world generally presents itself as very egocentric because life experience is limited to the current age. The idea of death is usually a very distant reality. Even if there are anxious thoughts about the possibility of parents dying first, it is usually not a topic that is comfortable to broach. It may surface somewhat through questions about the timing of mortality and what-ifs, but it is usually quickly assuaged by soliciting a promise from parents that they will never leave us or that there will always be an option to stay with them forever. When or if a pet dies it's often true that the burial process just happens and the pet "goes away" to a better place. Or a replacement pet fills the sad space and feelings of grief are slightly lessened so as not to dwell on painful aspects of the loss.

Distraction rather than openness, acceptance, and healing is often the knee-jerk coping mechanism of choice. It's nice to be insulated from discomfort and sadness but it is not always bene-ficial. Deep down there is a sense that the discomfort of loss and death are real but should not be acknowledged. Moving on gives the impression that little or no open communication about the loss will make the feelings go away and that sad is bad and happy is good. Internally we may feel off or anxious, but the subtle directive is to just go with the flow.

The initial experiences of death in our family were very tangible for me and not so much so for my kids at all. My first two kids had been born, and were very young, when I lost my maternal grandmother. She was ninety-three years of age so she lived a long and full life. She left this world with a clear mind and a strong will the day before George W. Bush was elected president. We were very close as she always took an active interest in communicating regularly and being openly authentic and giving. She was and remains to be an inspira-tion to me to this day. Her death was sad and left a gap inside our circle of family of origin and relatives. There was no question that I would fly across country to attend her funeral but it was the first time I would leave my two kids at home without me. So, death became another topic I introduced to my kids early on.

In the example of my grandmother it was a straightforward, somewhat standard conversation. I explained who she was in my life in reference to my mother being the grandmother of my own kids. I was able to tell them that she lived a long life, that I had a close relationship with her like they do with their grandma, and that she was at peace now that she had left the world. We discussed heaven and earth, through the basis of our personal beliefs and faith. It was an easy, direct conversation that helped explained why I was going on a trip for a short time. They had no memory of her so it didn't feel sad to them. It simply introduced the topic of death as part of the cycle of life.

However, the second experience with death impacting our family was not so straightforward. My sister and I were pregnant with boys at the same time. She was having her first child and I was having my third. It was the first time I found out ahead of time what the sex of my baby was going to be and it was my sister's choice to know all along. Our kids were to be roughly three months apart in age. At thirty-six weeks, through a series of events over the course of a few days, my sister found out that her little son, Noah, had several heart defects. The news was shocking as there was no indication of any concerns throughout her entire pregnancy. She remained in the hospital once she learned that fact and Noah was delivered by C-section on May 17, 2001. He graced the world for several precious hours and on the same day he arrived he left his physical body and was lifted away as an angel in heaven. He graces us now from above and has left his mark on all of us in some way.

The efforts of communication surrounding the ramifications of a death so different from the nature of my grandmother's passing were great. Reality, faith, prayer, relationship, will, energy, outlook, routine, and purpose were all compromised for me by Noah's death. It was a challenge to explain the situation to my kids because there was no viable meaning to any of it, but it was a necessary part of the process of facing reality and healing. Communication began as it did with my grandmother's death. Since my kids really did not know her I broached the subject in a similar way over the loss of Noah, who they really did not know as well. Everything else involving the circumstances and communication was completely different. My manner of explanation was much more emotional and was not a one-time communication. It was a topic of regular discussion because it greatly changed our lives. I was still carrying Shaun inside of me. My kids needed to know that the cousin they thought was going to join their lives on earth was now in heaven as we believe. They needed to understand displays of prolonged sadness, open emotion, and newly guarded thoughts and feelings.

The first year of Shaun's life in the world did not feel like a celebration in many ways. At his first birthday, where we always gather as an extended family, it felt like I was playacting and milestones to this day are internally bittersweet. We do celebrate Noah's birthday every year as extended family, too, so my kids needed to understand his death through this action as well. As they grew they could assimilate more, and even though death can be an uncomfortable and scary topic it is a part of life that impacts kids in many different ways. To hide from it doesn't truly protect as feelings surrounding death are ongoing and need to be processed and assimilated on an individual level. The stages of grief are not linear so the topic of death should be approached and faced with each person, not avoided. Work through feelings with children and show support through all the ups and downs of life. One of my relatives lost a spouse to suicide when my kids were teens. There was also a teenage boy in our town who lost his life in a fluke car accident. There have been other members of our community who lost their lives because of service in the military.

Most recently, my kids just lost their paternal grandmother to cancer. This is the closest they have come to losing a person in their lives with whom they had a tangible relationship. Due to the fact that we talk openly about the reality of death, the subject and feelings are not taboo to them. They can support their father openly, and they can ask for necessary support in return. They have material reminders that have been passed down to them from her that offer comfort and connection. My oldest son has a license plate of hers that he hung in his college dorm room. My daughter wears a ring of her grandmother's. My youngest son has several pictures that he keeps close as reminders of fun times from the past. There are many ways to process, comfort, and heal through the sad fact of death.

Odd as it may seem, the best method within the framework of MAPS is to participate in the experiences surrounding death. Death is a fact of life. The impact of death faces all of us at different times in different ways. I am not suggesting premature participation with the concept of death; the main idea is not to shy away from the truth when it does impact your kids in some way. Whether it be a distant relative, a friend, a pet, an acquaintance, a person of noto-riety, or an immediate loved one, the impact and the sadness are not something to shun or ignore. Teens especially are so vulnerable to broken connections, change, and feelings that even with something as uncomfortable as death they will welcome participation even when it seems they don't need the support. Take the initiative as a parent to broach the subject openly. Don't feel as though participating in communication requires thorough explanation. People who have lost loved ones have written about the awkwardness they feel when others do not acknowledge the straightforward reality of their loss and how they would have felt so much less alone if people were not afraid to express any open words of empathy.

Be simple in your efforts to sympathize, support, and be present frequently without the use of words, too. After pointedly expressing sorrow and empathy choose to continue to participate with actions. It's nice to feel the warmth of a hug, escape through a distraction, share space while working or resting, or do something active. Get out and change the scene a bit so that newness comes from the grief process as well. Talk about the cycle of life, the ritual of burial, the idea of reincarnation in all of its interpretations, and the myriad of feelings the stages of grief present. I liken the topic of death to puberty in the sense that everyone will experience it at some point but always in a very individual way. How we address it will depend on the age of our kids at the time the loss occurs but just like many of the stories I share throughout the book, our kids will take in only what they interpret at the time. We can never share too much because their brains will mitigate and form insights in the most appropriate way at that specific time. I have broached subjects with my kids way earlier that I anticipated when I envisioned being a parent and I have learned time and again that their minds automatically regulate and formulate the information in a way that makes sense on their level. What it does in the long run is provide them with necessary information to react and respond with confidence when various situations arise. Understanding comes through experience, which happens because of participation.

The most beneficial way to face the subject of death with teens is to participate through conversation, empathy, honesty, and openness. Tough subjects can be uncomfortable to broach and death is a highly charged matter that no one ever wants to voluntarily face. The reality of death can manifest fear, especially in younger kids, but a similar fear can manifest when there is no way to make sense out of something that doesn't seem quite right. When confrontation is glossed over kids can have a strong intuition about attempts to "cover up" and emotional insecurity is sure to follow. Be truthful in a compassionate way and participate in forming resiliency and strength through trial.

When parenting on the topic of death, it is best to contribute by a model of participation that teaches kids how to be the best version of themselves in every life circumstance. Use all your resources through belief systems, family, friends, support groups, books, writing, and the like. Participate through actions and nonverbal care. Show your emotions. Let your teens know that it is okay to be sad, that it is okay to grieve. Our kids need to see us experience a varied range of emotions, not just perennial happiness. Being happy is great and smiling is a wonderful practice but tears can be cathartic and healing if kids are not afraid to expose challenging emotions. Participate in the tough feelings with your kids and find some joy together, through the heartache. Externally processing will quell fears and foster a stronger sense of stability. Engage through your words, reach out by your actions, and always lead with love. By participating you will show your kids that wholeness can be attained even when it seems the situation is only full of brokenness. No one ever chooses to be touched by death but we always have a choice in how to respond. Get down in the trenches and crawl forward one step at a time.

ROAD MAPS

Do not shy away or try to cover up the topic of death. Participate and communicate with kids and lend nonverbal support. Remember that your kids will intuit if you are glossing over something or trying to cover up so if you are uncomfortable about the topic just let them know it's sad and not easy to discuss. Ask how you can support them and work together. It's ok to be challenged by loss. Death is a part of life. Everyone will go through the process in a different manner so educate yourself on the stages of grief. Let kids know that it is okay to feel sad over loss and that normal everyday life will be mixed with empty, uncomfortable feelings for a while. It may make sense to offer counseling options as mentioned in the chapter on divorce. The best advice is to participate even if that just means presence. Everyone experiences death at different times and in different ways so when it becomes necessary, just acknowledge this fact and support to the best of your ability.

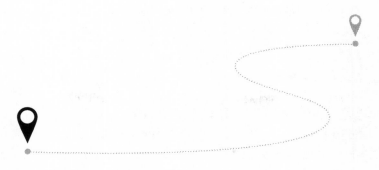

Closing

I hope you find some value in the concept of Life MAPS365. The idea has been a concept of mine for many years and now it is a way of life for me. My dream has been to write and publish a book and I could not be more proud of the subject matter for the topic. My kids are blessings beyond measure to me. This book simply highlights our relationships with one another. It is not meant to be preachy. I want it to be insightful and helpful. If anything, I hope that after reading it you will not think that it is necessarily unique advice at all and merely find it reinforcing. I just wished to offer some enjoyable, introspective ways to interact with and live healthy with your kids. I'm only an expert on the matter in that I believe wholeheartedly in the principles and I can show that they work. I can also tell you that they stand the test of time.

I now have two adult children who are no longer teenagers. The topics listed in this book and the conversations I continue to have with my kids are both the same and different. In the case of drugs and alcohol the core expectations are exactly the same, but the scenarios and legality are totally different. My oldest son is of legal drinking age. I still model acceptable drinking habits in his company. There is still no circumstance where it is appropriate for him or me to drink and drive. That line is still as clear as ever and it is one that I continue to uphold. Yet, I get to enjoy an occasional drink with him now. These past holidays I made a new drink called a "Peppermintini" and I made them for both of us while home enjoying a meal. My other kids took a taste of our drinks, but he and I each had two over the course of the meal and it was celebratory, enjoyable and perfectly appropriate. On a more humorous note, I blurred the legal line a bit with my daughter. She is a highly responsible, very self-aware, honest, twenty-year-old, sophomore in college. When I went to visit her over parents weekend this past year, we went out to dinner together, just the two of us. As we began to catch up in conversation, she became visibly uncomfortable and told me that she wanted to ask me something that might make her cry. I told her she could ask me anything and should not be uncomfortable. She didn't want the question to change my opinion of her and she was scared that it might. I told her that would never be the case. She had me on the edge of my seat. What she asked made me laugh out loud. She wanted to know if I would by her alcohol that she could keep and drink in her room with friends before going out to socials and/or parties. The reason why she was so nervous to ask is because she is my girl who always holds the line. She feels like she is an example to her younger brother, her nieces, and to many of her friends. She doesn't like to break rules and is not dishonest. She did not want to go behind my back to buy the alcohol but she didn't want to ask me and have me think less of her either. She is the one child I have who I trust to be wise about alcohol use. I know how closely she follows rules and takes pride in her character so, I would much rather have her ask me, buy the alcohol for her, and not have her get in trouble through a different route to the same end. I bought her some alcohol to keep in her room for special circumstances. I also reminded her that any consequence of action or reprimand was her own. As a side note, I told my oldest son and my daughter, at age 18, that any consequence from choices or behavior rested on them as a legal adult. There would be nothing to "fix" that they would not have to own as well. My daughter is open with her suitemates in college about her relationship with me and our conversations. I have been out with all of them for dinners and desserts when I am in town. They knew that I bought her the alcohol. When one of her suitemate's mom came into town the following weekend, she went in her daughter's closet and saw alcohol on the top shelf. She reprimanded her and asked questions about how she obtained it. In the girl's frustration, she blurted out to her mom, "Sarah's mom buys her alcohol and she is writing a parenting book!" When Sarah told me the story we both laughed and laughed. The statement is true but the reasoning has basis. I know I can trust my daughter with a small amount of alcohol. We talk every day since she has gone away to college. It has become a set pattern for us to check in and share parts of our days now that we are in separate states. I am her friend, now that she is an adult child, but I am also still her parent. I make decisions, on the basis of MAPS, by how I know her and who I want her to continue to become as she matures. This requires insight and trust. Insight from parenting her through her earlier years at home and trust to know that she is a young adult who needs to figure out healthy ways to make choices, mistakes, and decisions about how she will venture to live life independent from family.

My youngest, however, even though older at seventeen, is not quite to the point his older siblings are yet. He is not officially a legal adult. He is still living at home. He is finishing his senior year, applying for colleges, interested in playing soccer in college, has a girlfriend, has a car to use, and is well on the path to becoming independent from family. Since he is the youngest of three and we strive to foster healthy independence, he may have a slightly elevated sense of being able to make decisions without our consent. This happened in the case of a college recruitment email from a coach. The coach reached out to Shaun and copied me on the email. He had seen Shaun play at a showcase tournament even though the school was not one that Shaun was looking into. He was interested in Shaun as a player and wanted to know if Shaun was interested in talking to him and visiting the school. I read the email a couple days after it was sent (I am not the best at checking email) and when I brought it up to Shaun he told me he already told the coach he wasn't interested. This brought on several conversations which ultimately resulted in a positive outcome and became a learning point for all involved. I told him that he made a mistake in closing a door before it was even opened. I let him know that he did not have the authority to make a decision about college without talking to the people in his life who would be paying for his education. We discussed the school at length because he made some blanket statements about it that were not accurate so, we looked into it together and he found out that he didn't do adequate research before responding to the email. We both decided that it made sense to reach out to the coach again in an attempt to ride out the possibility of an opportunity by walking fully through the door. It worked in his favor, as he received a response that resulted in a great phone conversation with the coach. Now we just have to wait and see where the cards fall in the spring.

There are so many stages through the teen years. It's fun and exciting to watch your kids go from teenagers to young adults and beyond. The principles are always the same with MAPS but the dynamics shift.

I will say again that the principles stand the test of time. I am not the only one to stand by this fact: if you ask all of my kids, I know each one will say the same. I continue to have open lines of communication with each one of them. Always in their own ways, but always successfully. So ask and talk and let go. Live your best. Be open, honest, respectful, and kind. Take life for what it is worth. Take this book for what it is worth. I wish you all the best. I know we each make a difference when it comes to finding the way.

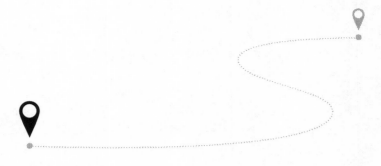

Acknowledgments

Writing a book has been a dream of mine for a long time. It is my ultimate dream to write several books and become a successful author by trade. There are a number of people I would like to acknowledge for ongoing support and inspiration through the process. There are people who I know intimately and those who motivate me through their own writing. Until I sat down to compose my gratitude, I did not realize that outside of my dedication, the individuals who foster my passion for writing are all women. To my aunt, Joan Falcone, who is the first person who asked to read the rough draft of my manuscript the second she learned that I was writing a book. To my sister, for whom no words can adequately express my admiration for her resilience, character and bond which has come full circle, and rests with me, in the best of places. To my cousin Sandi Burke, in whom I trust to the core. To my closest friends, though not an exhaustive list, for whom I must name, Debbie McBride, Lori Shellenberger, Laura Gorman, Michelle Pettit, Jadi Faul, Sarah Roughneen, Yvonne Ravad, and Robin Hansen, for their constant, selfless, practical and honest support throughout this entire journey. To the published authors, for whom I do not know personally, but who are my role models for authentic voice, I wish to thank Brene Brown, Joyce Maynard, Tosha Silver, Ann Lamott, Susie Walton, Barbara Ann Brennan, and Maria Shriver. To significant males in my life who allow and challenge me to see authenticity from a different gender perspective than my own, I must thank Connor Bodin, Stephen Ratliff, Rudy Delgado, Art Bollinger and Brian Johnson, for their friendship and willingness to engage in lengthy discussions that involve more listening than they may often choose. To Jared Kuritz, for believing in this dream of mine as much as I do, and seeing it through with me in an authentic, M.A.P.S.-filled, professional capacity. To Saint Therese, for her life and spirit through which the following words propel me forward in all my endeavors: She said, " May today there be peace within. May you trust that you are exactly where you are meant to be. May you not forget the infinite possibilities that are born of faith in yourself and others. May you use the gifts that you have received and pass on the love that has been given to you. May you be content with yourself just the way you are. Let this knowledge settle into your bones, and allow your soul the freedom to sing, dance, praise and love. It is there for each and every one of us." To my grandmother, Rose Dercole, for her life and spirit which live through me so, that I may aspire to embody her fortitude, up to the minute that she left this world, in such a way that she is remembered by all. And last, but certainly not least, to Betty Gallagher, who prays for me daily and has no prodding, obligation, or reason, other than her unconditional witness of the true love of Christ.

About the Author

Sheryl Matney holds a degree in Psychology which led her to non-profit work with young adults. She swapped careers to become a stay-at-home mom and raise three kids, Sam, Sarah and Shaun, into adulthood. As she reinvents herself once again, now that her kids are grown, it is her purpose to share the concept of MAPS, Model, Adapt, Participate and Slow Down, not just as a successful way to raise children, but as a holistic life practice which embodies her love of psychology and development. As a massage therapist (CMT), healing touch energy therapist, health coach and personal trainer, she brings mind, body and soul into her passion for writing and in her desire to foster vibrant potential for living at our best, through LifeMAPS365. She lives in Coronado, California, but is always ready for travel and adventure, wherever they may lead.

Made in the USA
San Bernardino, CA
21 August 2019